THE IMPACT OF
THE NORMAN CONQUEST

MAJOR ISSUES IN HISTORY

Editor
C. WARREN HOLLISTER,
University of California, Santa Barbara

The Twelfth-Century Renaissance
C. Warren Hollister

The Impact of Absolutism in France:
National Experience under Richelieu, Mazarin, and Louis XIV
William F. Church

The Impact of the Norman Conquest
C. Warren Hollister

The Commune of Paris, 1871
Roger L. Williams

Relativity Theory:
Its Origins and Impact on Modern Thought
L. Pearce Williams

THE IMPACT OF
THE NORMAN CONQUEST

EDITED BY

C. Warren Hollister

John Wiley & Sons, Inc.
New York   London   Sydney   Toronto

SERIES PREFACE

The reading program in a history survey course traditionally has consisted of a large two-volume textbook and, perhaps, a book of readings. This simple reading program requires few decisions and little imagination on the instructor's part, and tends to encourage in the student the virtue of careful memorization. Such programs are by no means things of the past, but they certainly do not represent the wave of the future.

The reading program in survey courses at many colleges and universities today is far more complex. At the risk of over-simplification, and allowing for many exceptions and overlaps, it can be divided into four categories: (1) textbook, (2) original source readings, (3) specialized historical essays and interpretive studies, and (4) historical problems.

After obtaining an overview of the course subject matter (textbook), sampling the original sources, and being exposed to selective examples of excellent modern historical writing (historical essays), the student can turn to the crucial task of weighing various possible interpretations of major historical issues. It is at this point that memory gives way to creative critical thought. The "problems approach," in other words, is the intellectual climax of a thoughtfully conceived reading program and is, indeed, the most characteristic of all approaches to historical pedagogy among the newer generation of college and university teachers.

The historical problems books currently available are many and varied. Why add to this information explosion? Because the Wiley Major Issues Series constitutes an endeavor to produce something new that will respond to pedagogical needs thus far unmet. First, it is a series of individual volumes—one per problem. Many good teachers would much prefer to select their own historical issues rather than be tied to an inflexible sequence of issues imposed by a publisher and bound together between two covers. Second, the Wiley Major Issues Series is based on the idea of approaching the significant problems of history through a deft interweaving of primary sources and secondary analysis, fused together by the skill of a scholar-editor. It is felt that the essence of a historical issue cannot be satisfactorily probed either by placing a body of undigested source materials into the hands of inexperienced students or by limiting these students to the controversial literature of modern scholars who debate the meaning of sources the student never sees. This series approaches historical problems by exposing students to both the finest historical thinking on the issue and some of the evidence on which this thinking is based. This synthetic approach should prove far more fruitful than either the raw-source approach or the exclusively second-hand approach, for it combines the advantages— and avoids the serious disadvantages—of both.

Finally, the editors of the individual volumes in the Major Issues Series have been chosen from among the ablest scholars in their fields. Rather than faceless referees, they are historians who know their issues from the inside and, in most instances, have themselves contributed significantly to the relevant scholarly literature. It has been the editorial policy of this series to permit the editor-scholars of the individual volumes the widest possible latitude both in formulating their topics and in organizing their materials. Their scholarly competence has been unquestioningly respected; they have been encouraged to approach the problems as they see fit. The titles and themes of the series volumes have been suggested in nearly every case by the scholar-editors themselves. The criteria have been (1) that the issue be of relevance to undergraduate lecture courses in history, and (2) that it be an issue which the scholar-editor knows thoroughly and in which he has done creative work. And, in general, the second criterion has been given precedence over the first. In short, the question "What are the significant historical issues today?" has been answered not by general editors or sales departments but by the scholar-teachers who are responsible for these volumes.

University of California,   *C. Warren Hollister*
Santa Barbara

CONTENTS

THE IMPACT OF
THE NORMAN CONQUEST

What was the effect of the introduction of feudalism by the Normans on the governance of England?

INTRODUCTION

To a modern American, the Norman Conquest of England may well seem so remote as to be almost unreal; but to an Englishman, who has only to look around him to see the castle mounds, the great square keeps, the massive-columned churches of the Norman age, the Conquest is apt to strike a deep emotional chord. Englishmen are inclined to take sides: to mourn the defeat of Harold, the last of the Saxon kings, or, in some instances, to rejoice in the victory of the Normans. Such partisanship can sometimes be detected even in scholarly writings on the Conquest, and the perceptive reader will discover that several of the essays reprinted in this volume disclose not only keen minds but potent emotions as well. And when a historian becomes a committed adherent of William the Conqueror or Harold Godwinson—of the "organizing genius" of the Normans or the rich culture and political traditions of the Anglo-Saxons—he is likely to react violently to historians who disagree with him. One's beloved is not to be insulted, and both love and hate have found their way into the historical controversy of the Norman Conquest.

Fundamentally, the problem of the Conquest is a problem of revolution *versus* evolution: did the Normans transform England or was their coming merely an episode in the development of British traditions? Admirers of the Normans are inclined toward the former view, admirers of the Anglo-Saxons toward the latter. But the question of continuity *versus* catastrophe is a genuine intellectual issue, the solution to which must depend on an exhaustive search and judicious interpretation of the evidence.

Did the Norman Conquest transform England? There can be no single answer, for the Normans affected some institutions and customs, and levels of society far more deeply than others. The question must be broken up into smaller questions: What was the Norman impact on the English peasantry and its institutions? On

I

towns and townsmen? On the Church? On the nobility? On the customs of aristocratic land tenure? On military tactics? On literature and thought? On art and architecture? The answers to some of these questions are relatively undisputed while others remain in a state of controversy. To further complicate the issue, the Norman Conquest of 1066 coincided with a great creative wave that was sweeping Europe in the mid-eleventh century. This was the advent of a period known as the High Middle Ages —a period that witnessed momentous transformations in economic and political organization, in thought, in literature and the arts, and in ecclesiastical reform and Christian piety. All Europe changed in the decades after about 1050: towns multiplied and commercial life intensified; vigorous new religious orders were formed and a powerful reform movement spread from papal Rome across the length and breadth of Europe; scholastic philosophy was born; Romanesque architecture reached its zenith and then evolved into the new Gothic style; agrarian productivity increased sharply; and the population soared. When such changes as these are noted in post-Conquest England it would be hazardous indeed to ascribe them entirely and simply to the Conquest.

Historians are agreed that since most of the Normans who came to England with William the Conqueror were members of a military aristocracy, the chief Norman impact is to be sought for in the area of aristocratic life and institutions. The Norman impact on agriculture, commerce, towns, and even ecclesiastical institutions, was probably not revolutionary; in some of these areas it may, indeed, have been relatively slight. But there can be no doubt that the aristocracy was transformed after 1066—that Frenchmen replaced Englishmen as the leading lay and ecclesiastical landholders and royal counselors. The key area of disagreement among historians is that of aristocratic *institutions:* Did the new Norman landholders hold their land, govern their subordinates, and perform their political and military obligations in the way that their Anglo-Saxon predecessors had done? Did they perform the traditional services for their land, or were new, typically Norman, services imposed? Was feudalism introduced into a previously nonfeudal land? These are the controversial issues in the modern historiography of the Conquest, and consequently they—and especially the problem of feudalism and military service—have been stressed in this volume.

The first three selections—excerpts from William of Malmesbury's *Deeds of the Kings of the English*, the *Anglo-Saxon Chronicle*, and the *Chronicle of Battle Abbey*—illustrate the reaction of three medieval writers to the Norman Conquest of England. The next selections introduce the reader to the two important nineteenth-century English scholars, E. A. Freeman and John Horace Round, in whose works and disputes the modern historical controversy is rooted. Freeman—Liberal, patriot, and Oxford professor—stressed the continuity of English traditions; Round—a Tory aristocrat and nonacademician—despised pre-Conquest Anglo-Saxon culture and regarded 1066 as the real beginning of English history. A third appraisal of the general significance of the Conquest, by Professor Frank Barlow of Exeter University, is a realistic, dispassionate modern study and an excellent example of current scholarly opinion.

The remainder of the volume focuses on the chief historical controversy relating to the Norman Conquest—the problem of feudalism. We encounter first the gradualist views expressed by the great nineteenth-century scholar, Bishop Stubbs, and then the more vigorous views of E. A. Freeman. The next selection is a series of excerpts from the uncompromising statement of the feudal revolution hypothesis written in the 1890's by the brilliant and flamboyant John Horace Round. After a decade or so of controversy, Round's views on the Norman origins of English feudalism came to be accepted by nearly every scholar and remained virtually undisputed throughout the first half of the twentieth century. Sir Frank Stenton epitomized Round's theory in the title of his important book, *The First Century of English Feudalism, 1066–1166* (1932), two passages from which are included here.

Since about mid-century, however, Round's feudal revolution hypothesis has been under attack; Freeman's theory of the continuity of English land tenure and military organization has undergone something of a renaissance. Round's own arguments were often highly technical, and his recent opponents have likewise based their arguments on detailed analysis of the historical evidence. Many of these arguments have to do with such recondite matters as scutage rates and the groupings of knight's fees and hides. (The hide is an Old English unit of land assessment which normally approximates 120 acres; it is a term to be remembered and cherished in these studies.) The controversial literature abounds in terminology that will be unfamiliar to the ordinary educated man; hence, many of the more technical aspects of the discussions have been eliminated from this introductory volume. The editor has sinned against several of the contributors by quoting their theories and excluding their documentation and some of their more technical analysis on the grounds that these passages would probably be unintelligible to the novice.

The controversy continues to this day, and the concluding selections in the volume exemplify the scholarly response to Round's attackers. There remain thoughtful scholars who reject the return to Freeman's "continuity." Some are actually angered by it. Others, drawing from each of the two schools of thought, are finding that the evidence discloses both Norman and Anglo-Saxon elements in the post-Conquest military-tenurial system. The final selection, by R. H. C. Davis, reminds us once again that the controversy over military tenures, hotly though it may rage, is, after all, only one limited issue in the larger problem of the Norman Conquest.

PART ONE

Contemporary Appraisals

1 FROM   *William of Malmesbury*
The Deeds of the Kings of the English

This monk-historian from Malmesbury wrote in the 1120's, 1130's, and 1140's, some two generations after the Conquest. He was a careful scholar and a historian of notable intellectual breadth. His picture of the moral decadence of the late-Anglo-Saxon England, however, is overdrawn.

Normans and Englishmen, spurred by different motives, have written of King William [I]. The former have praised him excessively, extolling to the utmost both his good and evil acts, whereas the latter, moved by patriotic hatred, have burdened their conqueror with undeserved condemnation. For my part, since the blood of both peoples flows in my veins, I will steer a middle course. When I am assured of his good deeds I will assert them openly. His evil conduct I will touch on lightly and sparingly, but not in such a way as to conceal it, so that neither will my history be condemned as false nor will I brand with ignominious opprobrium the man whose actions can almost entirely be reasonably excused, if not praised. Thus I will willingly and carefully tell such stories of him as may spur the lazy or instruct the enterprising, such stories as will be useful to the present age and pleasing to later ones. But I will spend little time with such matters as are of use to nobody and which evoke disgust in the reader and hostility toward the writer. There are always plenty of people ready to disparage the acts of noble men. My approach will be to extenuate evil as far as is consistent with truth and to forego excessive praise even toward good acts. I believe that all true judges will regard me, for this moderation, as neither timid nor blundering.

SOURCE. William of Malmesbury, *Gesta Regum Anglorum*, William Stubbs, ed., Rolls Series, No. 90, 1897–1899, Vol. II, pp. 283–284, 304-306, and 334–336.

. . . [The day of William the Conqueror's victory] was a fatal day for England, a sad havoc of our dear country brought about by its change of masters. For England had long before adopted the ways of the Angles which had varied according to the times. In the first years after their arrival they were barbarians in manner and appearance, warlike in their ways, heathens in their rites. But after embracing the faith of Christ, in time and by degrees, owing to the peace they enjoyed, they came to regard arms as merely a secondary matter and devoted their entire attention to religion. I speak not of the poor, who are often restrained by meanness of fortune from exceeding the bounds of justice. I exclude churchmen, who are restrained from leaving the true path, sometimes out of respect for their profession and sometimes from fear of shame. I speak of princes who, owing to the extensiveness of their power, are entirely free to indulge in pleasure. Some of these in their own land and some in Rome, changing their habit [becoming monks], gained a heavenly kingdom and communion with the saints. Many during their entire lives embraced the secular world only in outward appearance, so that they might spend their treasures on the poor or divide them among monasteries. What shall I say of the innumerable bishops, hermits, and abbots? Does the entire island not blaze with so many relics that you can scarcely pass through a village of any importance without hearing the name of some new saint? And how many others are unrecorded? With the passing of time, however, and for some years prior to the Normans' arrival, the love of learning and religion had decayed. Satisfied with only a modicum of education, the clergy could scarcely stammer the words of the sacraments, and anyone who understood grammar was an object of wonder and surprise. The monks made a mockery of their order's rule by wearing fine vestments and indulging in a great variety of food. The nobility, given up to luxury and lust, did not attend morning church as Christians do but carelessly heard matins and mass from a hurrying priest in their rooms amidst the seductive lures of their wives. The commoners, left unprotected, became a prey to the powerful who grew rich by seizing their property or selling them abroad as slaves, although it was characteristic of this people to prefer reveling to moneymaking. One repugnant custom which they adopted was to sell their female servants—when pregnant by them after they had sated their lust—either to public prostitution or to foreign slavery. Drinking parties were a universal practice in which they spent entire nights and days. They spent their entire fortunes on wretched and despicable houses, unlike the Normans and French who live frugally in noble and opulent mansions. The evil consequences of drunkenness followed in due course, and these, as everyone knows, weaken the mind. So it was that they engaged William recklessly and furiously rather than with military skill, and doomed themselves and their land to slavery by giving him an easy triumph in one single battle. "For nothing is less effective than rashness, and whatever begins with violence quickly ceases or is repelled." At that time the English wore short knee-length clothes. They had their hair cut short and their beards shaven, wore golden bracelets on their arms, and had their skin tatooed. They ate until they were stuffed and drank until they were sick. These last qualities they passed on to their conquerors; in other respects they adopted their conquerors' manners. But I would not want these evil customs ascribed to all Englishmen. I know that many churchmen at that time lived saintly and blameless lives. I know that many layman in this land, of all social ranks, were pleasing to God. Far be it from me to be unjust; my accusation is not against all. "But just as in peace God's mercy cherishes the good and the evil together, so too does his severity sometimes include them both in tribulation."

The Normans—that I may speak of them too—were, then as now, most proud in their dress and fastidious in their food, though not excessively so. They are a people accustomed to war and can scarcely live without it, fierce in charging against their foes and, when force fails, ready to use guile or seduce through bribery. As I have said, they live frugally in large houses. They envy their peers and wish to excel their superiors. They plunder their subjects although they defend them from others. They are faithful to their lords, but the slightest offense renders them treacherous. They weigh treachery by its chance of succeeding, and change their opinions for money. They are, however, the most courteous of peoples and hold foreigners in equal honor with themselves. Moreover, they intermarry with their subjects. Upon their arrival in England they revived religious observance which had become moribund there. One might then see churches arising in every village and abbeys in the cities and towns, constructed in a style previously unknown to the island. One might then see the land flourishing with a renewed observance of religion, so that every man of means regarded the day lost which he had failed to mark by some highly meritorious deed.

. . . King William [the Conqueror] graciously admitted men of foreign nations to his friendship, honored them without bias, and was devoted to almsgiving. Many English possessions he bestowed upon foreign churches, and his generosity—and that of his nobles—left scarcely an abbey neglected, particularly those in Normandy. Hence the poverty of Norman monasteries was mitigated by the wealth of England. In his days, therefore, the body of monks everywhere increased. Abbeys rose up that were ancient in rule but modern in architecture. But I now perceive the muttering of people who assert that it would have been preferable that the old buildings had been preserved in their pristine condition than that new ones should have been built from their plunder.

William was of proper stature, unusual corpulence, and fierce visage, his forehead bald, and of such immense strength of arm that people were often surprised that nobody could draw his bow, which he himself could bend while his steed was at full gallop. Standing or sitting he was a majestic figure of a man, although the protuberance of his stomach detracted from his royal appearance. Of splendid health, he was never confined with any serious illness until his last days. He was so devoted to the pleasures of hunting that . . . he allowed an area of many miles to become desolate, driving out the inhabitants, so that whenever he was free of other concerns he might pursue his pleasures there. He gave sumptuous, magnificent entertainments at the chief feast days. During the years that he could conveniently stay in England he passed Christmas at Gloucester, Easter at Winchester, and Pentecost at Westminster. At such times a royal order summoned to these places all the chief men of every social order, so that foreign envoys might be awed by the magnificence of the assemblage and the costliness of the feasts. At no other times was he more genial or magnanimous, so that the foreign visitors might proclaim far and wide that his generosity was equal to his wealth.

This style of feasting was always observed by his first successor but eschewed by his second.[1]

His eagerness for money is the one thing for which he can rightly be criticized. He sought all opportunities of accumulating it, regardless of means. He would say things and do things—indeed, almost anything, unbecoming though it was to his great royalty—when lured by the hope of money. I have absolutely no excuse to offer for this, unless it be, as has been said, that "One who is feared by many must necessarily fear many." For out of fear of his enemies he would empty the land of money to retard or turn back their onslaughts, frequently buying their forebearance with gold—as often happens in human affairs when strength fails. This shameful calamity prevails still and increases daily [under Henry I], so that both towns and churches are required to contribute. And this is not carried on by the imposters in full honesty; whoever offers the most wins the prize, all previous agreements being ignored.

2 FROM THE

Anglo-Saxon Chronicle
Peterborough Manuscript (E), A.D. 1087

The Anglo-Saxon Chronicle is actually a group of several distinct but related chronicles written in the Anglo-Saxon vernacular by unknown monks at various English abbeys. By A.D. 1080, however, all the separate Anglo-Saxon chronicles save one had been discontinued. The so-called "E" manuscript was carried on through the year 1154,

---

[1] William the Conqueror (King of England 1066–1087) was succeeded in turn by his two sons, William II, "Rufus," 1087–1100, and Henry I 1100–1135. A third son, Robert Curthose, succeeded to the duchy of Normandy on the Conqueror's death in 1087 but was defeated and imprisoned by Henry I in 1106.

SOURCE. John Earle and Charles Plummer, eds., *Two of the Saxon Chronicles Parallel*, Oxford: Clarendon Press, 1892, Vol. I, pp. 219–221. Reprinted by permission of the Clarendon Press, Oxford.

and it is this chronicle that is excerpted here. The excerpt below was probably written at a time when the manuscript was being compiled at St. Augustine's Abbey at Canterbury, but later, perhaps around 1122, the manuscript seems to have been moved north to Peterborough Abbey where it was kept current until the time of King Henry II's accession (1154).

The unknown author of the A.D. 1087 entry was evidently a thoughtful and perceptive man who had been at William I's court and endeavored to present an objective and rounded appraisal of the Conqueror and his impact on England.

Alas, how deceitful and transitory is this world's prosperity! He who once was a powerful king and a lord of many lands was left of all the land with nothing but seven feet, and he who once was bedecked with gold and with gems afterward lay covered over with earth.

He left three sons behind him. The eldest, called Robert, was duke of Normandy after him. The second, called William, wore the royal crown in England after him. The third, called Henry, was bequeathed innumerable treasures by his father.

If anyone wishes to know what kind of man he was or in what honor he was held or of how many lands he was the master, we will write of him even as we have known him—we who have ourselves looked upon him and at one time lived at his court. This King William was a man of great wisdom and power and surpassed all his predecessors in honor and strength. Although severe beyond all measure to those who opposed him, he was gentle to good men who loved God. On the very spot where God permitted him to conquer England he established a notable monastery and settled monks in it and endowed it generously. In his time the great cathedral at Canterbury was built, and many others, too, throughout all England. Moreover, this land was filled with monks living their lives according to St. Benedict's rule, and such was the state of Christianity in his time that everyone who wished, of whatever rank, could follow the monastic life. Furthermore he kept great state, wearing his crown thrice yearly whenever

he was in England. At Easter he wore it at Winchester, at Pentecost at Westminster, at Christmas at Gloucester, and at such times
all the leading men of England were with him: archbishops and
bishops, abbots and earls, thegns and knights. He was, moreover,
such a stern and ruthless man that nobody dared oppose his will.
Such earls as resisted him he kept in chains. He deprived bishops
of their sees and abbots of their abbacies, and cast thegns into
prison, and ultimately he spared not even Odo, his own brother.
Odo was a mighty bishop in Normandy—his cathedral church
was Bayeux—and he was the foremost man after the king, had an
earldom in England, and was the master of this country when the
king was in Normandy,[1] yet William had him imprisoned. Among
other things, one must not forget the good order that William
maintained in this land, to such a degree that any man of means
could travel unmolested across the country with his bosom full
of gold. No man dared kill another, no matter how the other
might have wronged him. And if any man fornicated with a
woman against her will he was promptly castrated.

*law of
William I.*

He ruled over England, and owing to his cleverness it was
surveyed so carefully that there was not a hide of land in England
of whose ownership and value he was ignorant, and these things
he set down in his [Domesday] survey. Wales was under his
dominion and he built castles there and thus he kept its people
entirely under his control.[2] Scotland, too, he reduced to subjection
through his great power.[3] The land of Normandy was his through
inheritance, and he ruled also over the county of Maine. Had he
lived only another two years he would have conquered Ireland
by his cunning and without any weapons. Without a doubt
people endured much oppression and a great many injuries in
his time:

> *He had castles built*
> *And severely oppressed the poor.*
> *The king was very stark*

[1] The reference here is to the Conqueror's half brother, Odo, bishop of
Bayeux and earl of Kent.
[2] An exaggeration; much of Wales remained effectively independent.
[3] Another exaggeration.

And took from his subjects many a mark
Of gold and hundreds of pounds more of silver.
These he took from his people by weight, and most unjustly,
With little need for such a deed.
He was sunk in avarice unseemly
And loved greed extremely,
He established a great deer preserve and imposed laws to pro-
    tect it,
Such that whoever slew a hart or hind
Was to be made blind.
He forbade the slaying of harts and boars
For he loved the stags as dearly
As if he were their father
Hares too, he decreed, should go unmolested.
The poor lamented and the rich protested,
But he was so ruthless that he minded not their hatred,
And they were forced to follow the king's will entirely,
If they would live or hold their lands—
Their lands or goods or the king's favor—
Alas, that any man should walk so proudly,
And exhalt himself and hold himself so far above others!
May almighty God have mercy on his soul,
And forgive him his sins!

These things we have written about him, good and evil alike, so that good men may emulate his virtues and utterly reject his wickedness and travel the path that leads us to the heavenly kingdom.

3   FROM THE
Chronicle of Battle Abbey

This chronicle probably postdates the Conquest by a little over a century. It reflects a far narrower, more parochial vision than the two previous ones. The unknown chronicler, looking at the Conqueror's career in retrospect, seems to believe that William's foremost achievement was the founding of three abbeys.

Let us now hasten briefly to recall to memory some things which we have omitted of the notable deeds of this glorious William, who was both in name and in reality a King.

This most noble prince founded three abbacies from his own estate, with competent lands attached to each, to say nothing of the innumerable possessions and benefices which, regarding his soul's prosperity, he gave, and permitted others to give, to various monasteries of the saints, both on this side the sea and beyond it. Two convents he built at Caen—one for monks, magnificent and wealthy, for himself, in which, as we have said, he was buried; and another for nuns, sufficiently notable, for the sake and at the instance of his queen Matilda, in which she lies honourably entombed. The third, which is the subject of our present narration, he founded in England, at the place where God had favoured him with victory.[1] And here, without doubt, it was his intention, had he died in England, to have been interred. But as he did not live to see it dedicated, he endowed it, alas! much less richly

[1] Battle Abbey. Unless otherwise indicated, this and subsequent footnotes are the editor's.

SOURCE. *The Chronicle of Battle Abbey*, M. A. Lower, tr., London: John Russell Smith, pp. 42–43; translated from *Chronicon monasterii de Bello*, J. S. Brewer, ed., London: Anglia Christiana Society, 1846.

than he had intended; for while it was yet incomplete, he had determined to make it, for greatness and wealth, one of the principal monasteries of England. Death, however, as we have seen, prevented this. From this circumstance let the wise man be admonished to do the good work he has proposed while he can, namely, today, since he knows not whether the morrow shall be granted him. It is wiser to avail ourselves of the present for a good deed, than to defer it to uncertainties; for we can rejoice more securely in praiseworthy deeds already performed, than in those which we have merely proposed, and which we know not whether we shall be able to accomplish. For it happens to some, that when with power to do good they defer its execution, the just judgment of God overtakes them for that sin (and every one is permitted to do that which is not expedient), and afterwards they want both the will and the opportunity. Still, however, as a good intention cannot be too much esteemed, this glorious monarch's liberal designs deserve the highest commendation; for laying the foundations of the abbey with a bountiful hand, he conferred so many gifts upon it, that if they be but well dispensed, they will prove sufficient for the inhabitants in all time to come. And although his unexpected decease must ever be a subject of regret for his Abbey, whose loss is not merely disadvantageous, but irreparable—a thing of which it is impossible to speak without lamentation—still, by the superintending providence of God over his servants, it has been sustained amidst all the vicissitudes of this world, by his authority and the liberality of his gifts; and thus far, through divine grace, it is defended and carried forward by the goodwill of his heirs.

PART TWO

General Modern Appraisals

1 FROM   *Edward A. Freeman*
The History of the Norman Conquest

This excerpt introduces us to the gradualist theory of the Norman Conquest, presented with erudition and literary skill by the great nineteenth-century scholar, Professor Edward A. Freeman, in his monumental six-volume history of the Norman Conquest (which actually runs from early Anglo-Saxon times through the thirteenth century). Freeman loved the pre-Conquest Anglo-Saxons and their last king, Harold Godwinson, who was vanquished at Hastings. Yet he also admired William and his Normans, and regarded the Conquest as an event of very great significance in English history—an event with creative and beneficent consequences which made England a finer land but did not transform it.

The Norman Conquest is the great turning point in the history of the English nation. Since the first settlement of the English in Britain, the introduction of Christianity is the only event which can compare with it in importance. And there is this wide difference between the two. The introduction of Christianity was an event which could hardly fail to happen sooner or later; in accepting the Gospel, the English only followed the same law which, sooner or later, affected all the Teutonic nations. But the Norman Conquest is something which stands without a parallel in any other Teutonic land. If that Conquest be only looked on in its true light, it is impossible to exaggerate its importance. And yet there is no event whose true nature has been more commonly and more utterly mistaken. No event is less fitted to be taken, as it so often has been taken, for the beginning of our national history. For its whole importance is not the importance which belongs to a beginning, but the importance which belongs to a

SOURCE. Edward A. Freeman, *The History of the Norman Conquest of England*, second edition, Oxford: The Clarendon Press, 1870–1879, Vol. I, pp. 1–5. Reprinted by permission of The Clarendon Press, Oxford.

turning point. The Norman Conquest brought with it a most
extensive foreign infusion, which affected our blood, our language, our laws, and our arts; still it was only an infusion; the
older and stronger elements still survived, and in the long run
they again made good their supremacy. So far from being the
beginning of our national history, the Norman Conquest was the
temporary overthrow of our national being. But it was only
a temporary overthrow. To a superficial observer the English
people might seem for a while to be wiped out of the roll-call
of the nations, or to exist only as the bondmen of foreign rulers
in their own land. But in a few generations we led captive our
conquerors; England was England once again, and the descendants
of the Norman invaders were found to be among the truest of
Englishmen. England may be as justly proud of rearing such
step-children as Simon of Montfort and Edward the First as of
being the natural mother of Ælfred and of Harold. In no part
of history can any event be truly understood without reference
to the events which went before it and which prepared the way
for it. But in no case is such reference more needful than in deal-
ing with an event like that with which we are now concerned.
The whole importance of the Norman Conquest consists in the
effect which it had on an existing nation, humbled indeed, but
neither wiped out nor utterly enslaved, in the changes which it
wrought in an existing constitution, which was by degrees greatly
modified, but which was never either wholly abolished or wholly
trampled under foot. William, King of the English, claimed to
reign as the lawful successor of the Kings of the English who
reigned before him. He claimed to inherit their rights, and he
professed to govern according to their laws. His position therefore, and the whole nature of the great revolution which he
wrought, are utterly unintelligible without a full understanding
of the state of things which he found existing. Even when one
nation actually displaces another, some knowledge of the condition of the displaced nation is necessary to understand the position of the displacing nation. The English Conquest of Britain
cannot be thoroughly understood without some knowledge of
the earlier history of the Celt and the Roman. But when there is
no displacement of a nation, when there is not even the utter
overthrow of a constitution, when there are only changes, how-

ever many and important, wrought in an existing system, a knowledge of the earlier state of things is an absolutely essential part of any knowledge of the later. The Norman Conquest of England is simply an insoluble puzzle without a clear notion of the condition of England and the English people at the time when the Conqueror and his followers first set foot upon our shores.

The Norman Conquest again is an event which stands by itself in the history of Europe. It took place at a transitional period in the world's development. Those elements, Roman and Teutonic, Imperial and Ecclesiastical, which stood, as it were, side by side in the system of the early middle age, were then being fused together into the later system of feudal, papal, crusading Europe. The Conquest itself was one of the most important steps in the change. A kingdom which had hitherto been purely Teutonic was brought within the sphere of the laws, the manners, the speech, of the Romance nations. At the very moment when Pope and Cæsar held each other in the death-grasp, a Church which had hitherto maintained a sort of insular and barbaric independence was brought into a far more intimate connexion with the Roman See. And as a conquest, compared with earlier and with later conquests, the Norman Conquest of England holds a middle position between the two classes, and shares somewhat of the nature of both. It was something less than such conquests as form the main subject of history during the great Wandering of the Nations.[1] It was something more than those political conquests which fill up too large a space in the history of modern times. It was much less than a national migration; it was much more than a mere change of frontier or of dynasty. It was not such a change as when the first English conquerors slew, expelled, or enslaved the whole nation of the vanquished Britons. It was not even such a change as when Goths or Burgundians sat down as a ruling people, preserving their own language and their own law, and leaving the language and law of Rome to the vanquished Romans. But it was a far greater change than commonly follows on the transfer of a province from one sovereign to another, or even on the forcible acquisition of a crown by an

---

[1] I.e., the Germanic invasions of the Roman Empire.

alien dynasty. The conquest of England by William wrought less immediate change than the conquest of Africa by Genseric;[2] it wrought a greater immediate change than the conquest of Sicily by Charles of Anjou.[3] It brought with it not only a new dynasty, but a new nobility; it did not expel or transplant the English nation or any part of it, but it gradually deprived the leading men and families of England of their lands and offices, and thrust them down into a secondary position under alien intruders. It did not at once sweep away the old laws and liberties of the land; but it at once changed the manner and spirit of their administration, and it opened the way for endless later changes in the laws themselves. It did not abolish the English language; but it brought in a new language by its side, which for a while supplanted it as the language of polite intercourse, and which did not yield to the reviving elder speech till it had affected it by the largest infusion that the vocabulary of one European tongue ever received from another. The most important of the formal changes in legislation, in language, in the system of government and in the tenure of land, were no immediate consequences of the Conquest, no mere innovations of the reign of William. They were the gradual developments of later times, when the Norman as well as the Englishman found himself under the yoke of a foreign master. The distinct changes in law and government which we commonly attribute to William the Norman gradually arose in the days of his successors, and they seem to have attained something like a definite shape under his great-grandson Henry the Angevin.[4] But the reign of William paved the way for all the later changes that were to come, and the immediate changes which he himself wrought were, after all, great and weighty. They were in truth none the less great and weighty because they affected the practical condition of the people far more than they affected its written laws and institu-

[2] Genseric, or Gaiseric, king of the Germanic Vandals, led his people into Roman North Africa in A. D. 429 and conquered it in the years immediately following.

[3] Charles of Anjou, younger brother of St. Louis of France, conquered southern Italy and Sicily in the later thirteenth century.

[4] King Henry II, A. D. 1154–1189.

tions. When a nation is driven to receive a foreigner as its King,
when that foreign King divides the highest offices and the greatest
estates of the land among his foreign followers, though such a
change must be carefully distinguished from changes in the written law, still the change is, for the time, practically the greatest
which a nation and its leaders can undergo.

2   FROM   *John Horace Round*
Feudal England

*This selection, characteristic of Round's writing, combines emotion
and technical scholarship in a highly distinctive brew. Unlike Freeman, Round wrote no lengthy books; his forte was the short technical
study. Some of the excerpts below appeared originally in articles published in the* English Historical Review *in the early 1890's—after Freeman's death—and were reprinted in 1895 in a collection of Round's
studies entitled* Feudal England. *Round was an unashamed admirer of
the nobility; he was, from the political standpoint, Freeman's opposite
—a Tory rather than a Liberal. He disliked Gladstone and Gladstonian
democracy and identified them in his mind with Harold Godwinson
and the "protodemocracy" of late-Saxon England. The pages below
betray an intense antagonism toward Harold, Freeman, and Gladstone
(whose name is never mentioned). To Round, the Norman Conquest
transformed England and was its salvation.*

It is probable that in spite of all the efforts of that school which
found in Mr. Freeman its ablest and most ardent leader, the "fatal
habit," as he termed it at the outset of his *magnum opus* "of
beginning the study of English history with the Norman Conquest itself," will continue, in practice, to prevail among those
who have a choice in the matter. It was characteristic of the late

SOURCE. John Horace Round, *Feudal England*, London: Sonnenschein &
Co., 1895, pp. 317–318 and 394–398.

Professor to assign the tendency he deplored to "a confused and unhappy nomenclature," for to him names, as I have elsewhere shown, were always of more importance than they are to the world at large. More to the point is the explanation given by Mr. Grant Allen, who attributes to the unfamiliar look of Anglo-Saxon appellatives the lack of interest shown in those who bore them. And yet there must be, surely, a deeper cause than this, an instinctive feeling that in England our consecutive political history does, in a sense, begin with the Norman Conquest. On the one hand it gave us, suddenly, a strong, purposeful monarchy; on the other it brought us men ready to record history, and to give us—treason though it be to say so—something better than the arid entries in our jejune native chronicle. We thus exchange aimless struggles, told in an uninviting fashion, for a great issue and a definite policy, on which we have at our disposal materials deserving of study. From the moment of the Conqueror's landing we trace a continuous history, and one that we can really work at in the light of chronicles and records. I begin these studies, therefore, with the Conquest, or rather with the coming of the Normans. For, as Mr. Freeman rightly insisted, it is with the reign of Edward the Confessor that "the Norman Conquest really begins"[1]: it was "his accession" that marked, in its results, "the first stage of the Conquest itself" . . .

"History is philosophy teaching by examples." In one sense the period of the Conquest was, as Mr. Freeman asserted in his preface, "a period of our history which is full alike of political instruction and of living personal interest." In one sense, it is an object-lesson never more urgently needed than it is at the present hour. Only that lesson is one which Mr. Freeman could never teach, because it is the bitterest commentary on the doctrines he most adored. In the hands of a patriot, in the hands of a writer who placed England before party, the tale might have burned like a beacon-fire, warning us that what happened in the past, might happen now, to-day. The Battle of Hastings has its moral and its moral is for us. An almost anarchical excess of liberty, the want of a strong centralized system, the absorption in party strife,

---

[1] King Edward the Confessor (A. D. 1042–1066) was reared in exile in Normandy and absorbed a great deal of Norman culture. After his coronation, Normans played an important role in the governance of England.

the belief that politics are statesmanship, and that oratory will save a people—these are the dangers of which it warns us, and to which the majority of Englishmen are subject now as then. But Mr. Freeman, like the Bourbons, never learnt, and never forgot. A democrat first, an historian afterwards, History was for him, unhappily, ever "past politics." If he worshipped Harold with a blind enthusiasm, it was chiefly because he was a *novus homo*,[2] "who reigned purely by the will of the people." He insisted that the English, on the hill of battle, were beaten through lack of discipline, through lack of obedience to their king; but he could not see that the system in which he gloried, a system which made the people "a co-ordinate authority" with their king, was the worst of all trainings for the hour of battle; he could not see that, like Poland, England fell, in large measure, from the want of a strong rule, and from excess of liberty. To him the voice of "a sovereign people" was "the most spirit-stirring of earthly sounds"; but it availed about as much to check the Norman Conquest as the fetish of an African savage, or the yells of Asiatic hordes. We trace in his history of Sicily the same blindness to fact. . . . But, in truth, the same excess of liberty that left England a prey to the Normans had left Sicily, in her day, a prey to Carthage: the same internal jealousies paralysed her strength. And yet he could not forgive Dionysius, the man who gave Sicily what she lacked, the rule of a "strong man armed," because, in a democrat's eyes, Dionysius was a "tyrant." That I am strictly just in my criticism of Mr. Freeman's attitude at the Conquest, is, I think, abundantly manifest, when even so ardent a democrat as Mr. Grant Allen admits that

". . . a people so helpless, so utterly anarchic, so incapable of united action, deserved to undergo a severe training from the hard taskmasters of Romance civilization. The nation remained, but it remained as a conquered race, to be drilled in the stern school of the conquerors."

2 "New man." Harold, who ruled England between January and October, 1066, was not a blood relative of Edward the Confessor or the previous Anglo-Saxon kings. He was earl of Wessex under Edward, and his sister was Edward's wife. Edward died childless in January, 1066, throwing the royal succession into dispute, and the English Witan (or royal council) chose Earl Harold, the most powerful man in the kingdom, to be king.

Such were the bitter fruits of Old-English freedom. And, in the teeth of this awful lesson, Mr. Freeman could still look back with longing to "a free and pure Teutonic England," could still exult in the thought that a democratic age is bringing England ever nearer to her state "before the Norman set foot upon her shores."[3]

But the school of which he was a champion has long seen its day. A reactionary movement, as has been pointed out by scholars in America, as in Russia has invaded the study of history, has assailed the supremacy of the Liberal school, and has begun to preach, as the teaching of the past, the dangers of unfettered freedom.

Politics are not statesmanship. Mr. Freeman confused the two. There rang from his successor a truer note when, as he traversed the seas that bind the links of the Empire, he penned those words that appeal to the sons of an imperial race, sunk in the strife of parties or the politics of a parish pump, to rise to the level of their high inheritance among the nations of the earth. What was the Empire, what was India—we all remember that historic phrase—to one whose ideal, it would seem, of statesmanship was that of an orator in Hyde Park? Godwine,[4] the ambitious, the unscrupulous agitator, is always for him "the great deliverer." Whether in the Sicily of the "tyrants," or the England of Edward the Confessor, we are presented, under the guise of history, with a glorification of demagogy.

"No man ever deserved a higher or a more lasting place in national gratitude than the first man who, being neither King nor Priest, stands forth in English history as endowed with all the highest attributes of the statesman. In him, in those distant times, we can revere the great minister, the unrivalled parliamentary leader, the man who could sway councils and assemblies at his will, etc., etc."

We know of whom the writer was thinking, when he praised that "irresistible tongue"; he had surely before him a living model,

[3] Both Freeman and Round appear to agree that pre-Conquest England was "democratic" or "protodemocratic." This is an interpretation which no modern scholar would accept.

[4] Godwine or Godwin was King Harold's father and predecessor as earl of Wessex.

who, if not a statesman, was, no doubt, an "unrivalled parliamentary leader." Do we not recognise the portrait?—

"The mighty voice, the speaking look and gesture of that old man eloquent, could again sway assemblies of Englishmen at his will.

"The voice which had so often swayed assemblies of Englishmen, was heard once more in all the fulness of its eloquence."[5]

But it was not an "irresistible tongue," nor "the harangue of a practised orator," of which England stood in need. Forts and soldiers, not tongues, are England's want now as then. But to the late Regius Professor, if there was one thing more hateful than "castles," more hateful even than hereditary rule, it was a standing army. When the Franco-German war had made us look to our harness, he set himself at once, with superb blindness, to sneer at what he termed "the panic," to suggest the application of democracy to the army, and to express his characteristic aversion to the thought of "an officer and a gentleman." How could such a writer teach the lesson of the Norman Conquest?

"The long, long canker of peace" had done its work. . . . The land was ripe for the invader, and a saviour of Society was at hand. While our fathers were playing at democracy, watching the strife of rival houses, as men might now watch the contest of rival parties, the terrible Duke of the Normans was girding himself for war.

[5] Round is suggesting that Freeman had Gladstone in mind when writing of Harold.

3   FROM   *Frank Barlow*
      "The Effects of the Norman Conquest"

Frank Barlow, professor of history at the University of Exeter, is a modern scholar who has made important contributions to our understanding of Edward the Confessor, William the Conqueror, and the Norman Conquest. He is also an expert on the medieval English Church. In the selection below he presents a sound modern interpretation of the effects of the Conquest—an interpretation that, in its objectiveness and emotional neutrality, contrasts sharply with the writings of both Freeman and Round.

The longest, most elaborate and most detailed account of the Conquest is E. A. Freeman's *The History of the Norman Conquest, Its Causes and Its Results,* published in six large quarto volumes between 1867 and 1879, and containing well over a million words. General Patton perused it before D-day in 1944, ostensibly to find out which roads William had used in Normandy and Brittany, although possibly as a soporific; but it is now not much read. Nevertheless its influence has been profound.

Freeman believed in the fundamental continuity of English history from Æthelberht to Albert, and in his book started with the Germanic settlements in Britain in the fifth century, and finished with "the emergence of a national state" under Edward I. He asserted, "The great truth . . . that the importance of the Norman conquest is not the importance either of a beginning or

SOURCE. Frank Barlow, "The Effects of the Norman Conquest," in C. T. Chevallier, ed., *The Norman Conquest: Its Setting and Impact,* London: Eyre and Spottiswoode, 1966, pp. 125–128, 131, 133, 135–138, 140–145, 147–148, 150–154, and 156–161. copyright © 1966 by Frank Barlow. This selection from *The Norman Conquest* by Dorothy Whitelock, David C. Douglas, Charles H. Lemmon, and Frank Barlow is reprinted with the permission of Charles Scribner's Sons, Eyre and Spottiswoode, and the author.

of an ending, but the importance of a turning point." He believed
that the Conquest did no more than give a twist to the gradual
elaboration of political institutions implicit in primitive Germanic
society. He did not regard the Conquest—at least in the long
view—as harmful. It taught the English to know themselves, to
refine their virtues and enabled them to re-emerge and collaborate
with a noble king in establishing parliamentary government. Freeman wrote, "The fiery trial which England went through was
a fire which did not destroy, but only purified. She came forth
once more the England of old. She came forth with her ancient
laws formed into shapes better suited to changed times, and with
a new body of fellow workers in those long-estranged kinsmen
whom birth on her soil had changed into kinsmen again."

One scholar, however, was not impressed. J. H. Round, working in a much narrower field, primarily that of genealogy and
local history, and irritated by the great assumptions and inaccurate
detail, the haziness at critical points and, perhaps, the arrogant
tediousness of Freeman's vast canvas, offered a cataclysmic view
of the Conquest which found favour for a time. He disliked what
little he knew of Old-English history, was authoritarian in politics
and had the "snob-values" of the genealogist and antiquarian. For
him it was inconceivable that England's virtues could have sprung
from that Germanic morass. "There must be, surely," he wrote,
"an instinctive feeling that in England our consecutive political
history does, in a sense, begin with the Norman Conquest." This
protest against nineteenth-century evolutionary views had its
effect and a generation of scholars backed Round against Freeman. There was, they maintained, a real and profound break in the
continuity of English history. The origin of many, if not most,
medieval English governmental and social institutions must be
sought in Normandy and France and not in the Old-English
kingdom.

Yet historical opinion has veered again. Round's attack, although
devastating, was on a narrow front. It was possible to re-form
the line. Today, once more, students of English kingship and
government, of the English church and of English economic
history will assume at least basic continuity from the Old-English
to the Anglo-Norman kingdom, and will look to the Norman
duchy mainly for the influences that in the later eleventh century

modified the indigenous pattern. Moreover, they will distinguish between the purely Norman contribution and those ideas and fashions whose entry was simply facilitated by the Conquest. The Normans not only brought in foreign wares but remained active carriers of them.

Also there has been a tendency among historians to recover Freeman's width of vision, his ability to see England as part of Europe and Christendom, and Normandy within the framework of the Frankish kingdom. Differences in their institutions and cultures are now often regarded as variations within a common sociological system. Such a view permits intricate and delicate inter-reactions to occur when different regional and national customs are brought together.

The historian's position, however, is not exactly as it was. Incessant research in a subject which has continued to hold the interest of scholars, has produced a knowledge and understanding of the Old-English kingdom, the duchy of Normandy and the Anglo-Norman kingdom far more exact in detail than was possible in Freeman's day. Some problems have been reexamined time after time, most fruitfully when there has been a true appreciation of current European scholarship. English history cannot usefully be studied outside its context. Hence, although there is still much conflict of view, and still room for the individual interpretation, the factual basis is firmer and the scale of disagreement has diminished.

Norman apologists, like William of Poitiers, the duke's panegyrist, maintained that William's sole interest in England, as earlier in Maine, was to obtain and hold his just inheritance against wrongful claimants. The legal and moral strength of William's case need not be discussed here. But we must allow him a case and an intention to operate within his ideas of law and justice. There is, therefore, much to be said for the view that William's original, and always basic, purpose was to slip into the shoes of his kinsman, Edward, and to take over his inheritance as a going concern. He would be prepared for some opposition, some disturbances. He would know that he would have to make some changes in order to secure his rule. But he would not expect to be disappointed in the value of the legacy. A crown and the traditional rights and revenues of the English king were as much as any heir could have desired. If Harold had not broken faith and opposed him, or if English resistance had then ceased, it is likely that William would have ruled in England, as in Maine, indeed as in all his dominions, essentially content with his inherited legal rights.

Although this attitude was distorted by events, it was never completely transformed. William developed no great liking for England or its inhabitants. He soon gave up his intention to learn the language. He only resided in the kingdom when it was necessary to see to its good order or defence. To the very end William grudged the drain on his time and energy that English complications caused. He was much happier fighting on his ducal frontiers. When he bequeathed Normandy to his eldest son,[1] and England to his second son, William Rufus, he thereby broke up his empire—without a pang. We should not, therefore, imagine that the Conqueror had any premeditated or deliberate intention to make drastic changes in the English kingdom. He invaded to acquire a throne and its revenue, and with them dignity and glory. . . .

Yet there was one special feature of Norman rule which could not easily be forgotten in what remained of the higher strata of English society. Even more shameful than the humiliations of the war was the disgrace that followed, especially the denial to the natives of high office. . . .

The English remained depressed because within a decade of the battle of Hastings the Anglo-Danish aristocracy, both ecclesiastical and lay, had been replaced by another which considered itself French. This was the field in which J. H. Round worked; and he had every reason to point to a revolution. All the men who had been great in King Edward's reign and most of the lesser nobility had been swept away. After the battle and rebellions William, whether he had wanted it or not, had the whole of England at his disposal. What is more, the native nobility had to be replaced. William could not have administered the entire kingdom through officials; and his followers would not have tolerated such greed. The new king reserved to himself an enormous de-

[1] Robert Curthose, duke of Normandy 1087–1106.

mesne, about a fifth of the arable area, and out of the rest rewarded his kinsmen, vassals and others who had a claim on his bounty. . . .

The redistribution of the lands of England among the French was both a grant of revenue and a military occupation. The new landholders acquired all the rents and services which their predecessors had enjoyed. In an economic context the change of lords made little difference to the agricultural producers, the farmers and their labourers, the small-holders and the stock breeders. There were many rough actions and misunderstandings; there may occasionally have been new men with new ideas. Sometimes there was a determined effort to restock under-exploited estates. There may have been a general movement to require full economic rents. But the incoming lords, certainly the major barons, were mostly absentees. The men who enjoyed William's greatest trust, and received the largest estates in England, he used as his captains in the Norman wars. These may have pressed heavily on their stewards, reeves and other agents to increase the revenues from their estates; but they had no revolutionary means of exploitation.

More noticeable in the countryside was the military aspect of lordship. The English nobles' had kept retainers, who rode and on occasion fought beside them. Often these vassals held or were granted land. But English halls were defended only by a ditch and palisade or hedge. The lords had no true military strongholds. The Conquest made a great change. William built castles in the more important towns to hold royal garrisons and enable his armies to move in stages throughout the kingdom. His vassals built private castles to protect their estates. Under Stephen, the last of the Norman kings,[2] a new wave of castle-building spread through the country, a result of the civil wars. These baronial castles were mostly simple constructions of earth and timber and were often allowed to decay in peaceful times. But a new feature, the basin-like mound of the motte, had been added to the English landscape.

[2] Stephen, who reigned from 1135 to 1154, was succeeded by Henry I's grandson, Henry II, product of the marriage between Henry I's daughter Matilda and Geoffrey of Anjou. Henry II is commonly regarded as the first of the Angevin Kings of England.

The replacement of an Anglo-Danish by a French aristocracy was bound to affect the social customs in the kingdom. It is true that the Norman, Breton, Flemish and other French barons were, in education, interests and outlook, not unlike the thegns and earls whom they replaced. A few Normans and Bretons had settled in England during Edward's reign; Earl Harold had probably not felt a complete stranger in William's army when he joined the duke for the Breton campaign of 1064. There were many minor differences in the social conventions, and there was the barrier of language; but there was no greater cleavage in culture—indeed probably less—than, say, between English and Norman landlords today. . . .

Yet French customs did not yield as quickly as Scandinavian in the past. There was the absence of English social equals. The English language was spoken by inferiors and sounded barbarous to the French. English personal names especially were considered ridiculous and uncouth. Conversely the conquered were soon tempted to imitate the new aristocracy. English parents began to give their children Norman names. All with social pretensions who came in contact with the foreigners aspired to speak French. On most large estates there remained a number of Englishmen in the class between the newcomers and the farmers—"squires" with modest estates. These were to be the intermediaries, bi-lingual, but with English as the cradle tongue, and often aspiring to marry into the middle or lower strata of Norman society. There were also the less privileged Normans, priests and servants, who were glad to marry English women. In mercantile society there was little prejudice on either side. But if such contacts eased the recovery of English culture they also more effectively helped the spread of French. To behave like the French had become the mark of gentility.

Throughout the Norman period, therefore, the French formed a fairly exclusive circle. It is possible that Henry I and his nephew, Stephen, could understand a little English; but they did not speak it: they had no need to. When William II took over the duchy of Normandy, when Henry I conquered it, when Stephen of Blois, count of Mortain and Boulogne, became king, when Matilda, countess of Anjou, invaded, there were new influxes of foreigners. The oldest established colonists were settling down, racial antagonism was dying fast, but there was enough renewal of French influence at the top to keep the new culture alive.

The Norman settlers brought their laws and customs with them and had no wish for change. All who received a grant of land took it as a fief held on conditions, and acknowledged that they were the vassals of the donor. It does not seem that the early grants were normally made in writing, by charter, or that the conditions of tenure were explicitly rehearsed. We may assume that the grantor expected the grantee to perform all the services for which the land was traditionally liable and also the duties of a vassal as generally understood at the time. The vassal would owe his lord fealty and loyalty, service in his court, escort and defence duties, and would fight under his lord's flag on military campaign. The lord and his vassals formed a family: each owed the other comfort and protection. The vassal was expected to aid his lord in every way, and the lord was required to watch over his vassal's interests, and make provision for his widow or orphaned children. The act of homage and the oath of fealty created a social bond. . . .

One of the great effects of the Conquest . . . was the creation of a new body of law in the kingdom. As it was formed by the French, and at first affected few who were not French, it owed little directly to the English past, although it should not be regarded as something completely alien. A Harold or a Leofric could have quickly adjusted himself to the new society and would not necessarily have found its rules uncongenial. It owed much to Norman and French custom; but it was made in England to meet English conditions. A branch of it, the law of the king's court, became eventually the common law of the land. Yet the king's justices often declared the law when on eyre in the shire court, where Old-English law ran; and when we trace the later history of English law it is difficult to be sure what contribution, either in substance or in procedure, was made by the Normans. We can point to minor features, such as the *duellum* (ordeal by combat), and pleading in French. But it would be rash to hold that important principles of twelfth- and thirteenth-century English law, such as the indefeasibility of private rights, the importance of possession, the necessity for a just judgement of a court before execution of sentence and judgement by peers, were more

Norman than English in origin. Nor can some vital procedural habits, such as the original writ or trial by jury, be assigned an exclusive Norman provenance. In any case they were not the inventions of the honorial[3] courts.

When we pass from law to social attitudes we enter an even less tangible world. One military society, with basically northern traditions, had been replaced by another which had imitated its customs from France. There were differences between the two, and, although all attempts to portray them tend to become caricatures, we can do no more than generalize. The Old-English nobility had been nurtured more comfortably. There was a tradition of literacy among them and, in the eleventh century, a fondness for luxury. Men wore their hair long and cultivated social graces. The Bayeux Tapestry depicts their elegance. The Normans, although they took pride in their dress and food, were rougher, less cultured, less sophisticated. At first they considered their crudity a virtue and mocked at the English nobles whom they thought as beautiful as girls. But with English wealth they soon aped some English fashions, and by William II's reign moralists were denouncing their effeminacy. The two races had a different attitude towards women. In Anglo-Saxon society women were held in typical northern respect. They held land and could leave it by will. Norman society was more masculine; manners were those of the camp and castle. William I showed small interest in women; William Rufus was a homosexual; and Henry I, although a lecher, was said to take no pleasure in his mistresses. A few ladies made their mark in this rough world, but only by displaying masculine virtues.

Within half a century of the Conquest, however, some of these attitudes were disappearing among the Normans. It was not unusual for the grandsons, and especially the granddaughters, of the Domesday baronage[4] to receive some education. During the course of the twelfth century women began to cultivate their own interests and to have influence over men. We notice the first faint effects of courtly love and of the French romance. Society

---

[3] I.e., baronial or feudal courts, as distinct from royal courts and the folk courts of shire and hundred.

[4] I.e., the barons at the time of the Domesday survey, A. D. 1086.

manners would not have developed in quite the same way if the
aristocracy had remained English or if the newcomers had adopted
the vernacular speech. But the Norman contribution was to provide the vehicle, the language, for the new ideas rather than the
ideas themselves. It is difficult to point to any strand in gentility
which was purely Norman. The standards were French, and
remained so under the Angevins.

Within and above the feudal society was the king. William I
had no direct experience of strong monarchy. He was familiar
with some aspects of royalty through his close contact with his
weak Capetian overlord; and he was aware that there were
stronger kings in Germany and England. With such a background
he must have viewed the rights of an English king as something
to grasp and retain, not as something in obvious need of reform.
Nevertheless, between 1066 and 1154 the royal administration
changed considerably in detail. Changes would have occurred
without the Norman conquest. Royal government had made
amazing strides in England between 899 and 1066 and there is no
reason to suppose that stagnation would have set in with the
accession of Harold. Moreover, few of the innovations can be
assigned a purely Norman origin or attributed to characteristic
Norman genius. They were mostly demanded by alterations in
the circumstances. Norman achievement was to re-establish traditional English monarchy, modify it to suit the new conditions
and develop it pragmatically as need arose. . . .

The most obvious effect of the Norman conquest was that
the king became a frequent absentee. English kings, except Cnut,
had hitherto always resided in the kingdom. William and his
successors, when they were also duke of Normandy and count
of Maine, had to make provision for the government of England
to continue in their absence. The natural arrangement would
have been for a member of the royal family, assisted by a baronial council, to act as regent. William I made such a provision
for Normandy and Henry I occasionally for England. But as
the Conqueror had no kinsman to whom he wanted to entrust
England, and William II was unmarried, the important tradition
was created that the king could be represented by one of his
servants, normally a bishop. Henry I gave this arrangement in-

stitutional form. About 1109, soon after he had dispossessed his brother of Normandy, he appointed standing deputies, with the title of justiciar, in both England and Normandy, and for each he created a fixed local court, which became known as the English or Norman exchequer. Roger le Poer, a chaplain who had been trained in Henry's household, and had risen to be royal chancellor and then bishop of Salisbury, was the first holder of the office in England. His opposite number in Normandy was John, bishop of Lisieux. Both these men, through sons or nephews, founded clerical dynasties which were to give the monarchy devoted service and facilitate the continuity of the administration into the Angevin period. . . .

The other most obvious effect of the Conquest was the re-endowment of the monarchy. Owing to the demands made on royal generosity and the need to reward servants, royal demesne tended to diminish. Kings became entitled to services, which could not always be enforced, instead of revenue with which services could be hired. Hereditary monarchies were usually in the end starved out. Changes of dynasty enriched the monarchy, for the new king added his private estates to the royal demesne, although, if the usurper was weak, he had many debts to repay, much loyalty to buy. In 1066 Harold restored the royal demesne by adding Wessex. William through confiscation did even better. Then, under his two sons, the process was reversed until Stephen contributed his own and his wife's English estates. Stephen, however, was by nature and necessity generous. . . .

The broad pattern of royal financial administration remained unchanged from the Old-English period. It was vital that there should be proper audit at all levels; and the one clear innovation in the Norman period was Henry I's decision that the justiciars should audit the accounts of some of the royal financial agents in their exchequer court. Records of some aspects of the audit, especially of outstanding debts and judicial decisions on fiscal matters, were kept; and the English Pipe Rolls, of which one example survives from the reign of Henry I, form one of the earliest and longest-running series of royal records.

The existence of these rolls and the *mystique* of the exchequer auditing procedure have, however, led to a common misunderstanding of Norman and Angevin royal finance and have often

created the impression that it was more sophisticated than it
really was. In fact, by 1135 no substantial advance had been made
on Anglo-Saxon practice. All royal moneys were the king's and
for and at his pleasure. His chamber, in which he kept his spend-
ing money, remained, therefore, at the centre of the system. For
the king the importance of the English and Norman exchequers
in this capacity was simply that they squeezed every penny out
of his debtors. For us they are proof that Henry I and his advisers
could improve the administrative machinery by introducing the
best techniques available at the time.

As the Norman kings were wealthy they were less dependent
than many of their contemporaries on the physical services of
their vassals. In England the Conqueror was at first short of
troops; and in the years of turmoil every soldier who could be
raised was required for indefinite periods of service. Although
William and his principal captains usually commanded mercenary
armies, the new earls and barons were obliged to call out not
only their own vassals but also those Englishmen who owed
the king military service. William had Englishmen in his army
as early as 1067 and later they fought in France and Maine.
Barons were encouraged to build castles and recruit soldiers to
garrison them. For at least a decade the Normans organized themselves for war. Once order had been re-established, however, both
the king and his barons began to lose interest in these special arrangements. The barons counted the cost. The king still needed
the services of his barons, but more discriminately. He kept his
most important English barons and some of their forces with him
on the Continent; in England he appointed bishops as his deputy
military commanders and reduced the army to little above min-
imum garrison strength. In 1085, when a Danish invasion threatened, he had to bring a large mercenary force to England. . . .

One immediate effect of the Conquest was an increase in dis-
order, crime and disputes over land. William used every available
method to keep the courts working. He guaranteed to each race
its own law, confirmed to every man his just rights and made
provision for a conflict of laws. The king and his barons held
courts for their own vassals; but it was essential that the territorial
courts—shire, hundred and "manorial"—should continue to func-
tion, for it was in these that English law ran. By 1072 the ranks

of the shire thegns, the men who knew the law and the history of estates, was thinned, and William improvised to keep the local courts running: meetings of groups of shires or hundreds were convoked, judges appointed to oversee several shires, judges dispatched from the royal court to hear an important case in the locality, local justiciars appointed to help the sheriff in judicial work. In time barons and knights of French descent learned their duties as suitors and judges in the shire court. Too much attention can be given to the, almost invisible, honorial courts: their jurisdiction was largely confined to domestic disputes. The shire and hundred courts remained the basic tribunals.

Once the Norman kings had embarked on the policy of maintaining the old local courts and keeping the honorial courts in check, they had to develop the judicial functions of their own *curia*. It had to be more than the court for the king's own vassals; it had to oversee and supplement the local courts, to take ultimate responsibility for the dispensation of justice throughout the kingdom. In this policy Norman aims and Old-English practice came together, and interesting developments took place, especially under Henry I.

Henry not only took new steps to reanimate the local courts, and increased the judicial activities of his own, but also brought the two into powerful conjunction. On his side he created the justiciar and his exchequer court and as well sent judges on general eyre through the kingdom. These men visited the county courts, where the hundreds were represented, scrutinized their conduct, heard criminal cases reserved to the king (the pleas of the crown), investigated all categories of royal rights and heard important land cases, or common pleas as they came to be called. Most cases were still heard in the local courts, whether territorial or seigneurial; but important cases, and especially those in which the king had an interest, could be heard before the king's justices in eyre, before the justiciar at the exchequer or by the king himself. It was a flexible, simple system. There was one royal court, dividing and re-forming according to convenience, and capable of reaching out into almost every locality. The same royal justices sat with the king or the justiciar and went on eyre. They were not professionals, but omni-competent royal servants; yet most future juridical developments were already present in germ. Cases were being originated by obtaining a royal writ; juries of presentment and trial juries were being sworn. Juries are often regarded as a Norman innovation imitated from Frankish practice. It is a very dark subject. But we should notice that English juries are most in evidence when the ancient courts of shire and hundred meet royal judges. Although the king and his justices may have moulded the pattern, the sworn evidence of local communities seems to have been an Old-English as well as a Frankish custom.

William I and his sons exploited English kingship to the best of their ability. Although some historians have regarded it as a new monarchy, it is doubtful whether the Normans contributed any completely new strand. Lordship was nothing new. No new struggle for power, with the king allying with the English against his barons, came suddenly into existence. The interests of the king and his barons were not basically opposed: normally they shared a class, even a family, interest. It is true that individual barons resented the king's use of his power, and on the death of each king there was a general reaction against strong rule. Such outbursts were not new in English history. It is also true that the English looked to the king against local oppression and in moments of crisis would support him against aristocratic rebellion; but that too had been a feature of the past. This is not to say that there was no change. With both the monarchy and the nobility strengthened there was more chance of conflict; and there began that running debate between the king and his barons over rights and duties which led to a constitution. The charter extorted by the barons and church from Henry I at his coronation, promising relief from the bad customs introduced by his brother, even if ineffective at the time, proved to be an important precedent. However traditional the powers wielded by the Norman kings may have been, they were given new impetus, a special development, a Norman interpretation. But no Norman king based a claim on the ducal past. All men looked to the laws of King Edward. . . .

After the Conquest the English church, with a long, unbroken history and deep-seated insular customs, rich, artistic, unique in its vernacular culture, was viewed with largely hostile eyes by men educated in another tradition. As a result there was considerable change. But again it was a complex process. As there were already in the English church several foreign bishops and abbots besides Englishmen anxious for reform, and the Norman church itself was ruled to an even greater degree by foreigners, there could be no simple confrontation of English and Norman ideals. Moreover, most of the more important developments in the English church after 1066 were not of Norman inspiration. The new factors, such as the growth of papal monarchy and the rising standards in education, would have affected England whatever the political events might have been.

The immediate Norman attitude towards the church they found was extremely mixed. Although they were awed by its splendour, they despised its customs and culture, and also coveted its wealth. They disliked its archaic Roman liturgy, its buildings in an outmoded style and its incomprehensible learning. Moreover, William had clerical claimants on his generosity and himself wanted bishops whom he could trust absolutely, who could serve as his vice-regents in the kingdom. The answer was reform, for this could cover all motives. In 1070 William, through papal connivance, secured the legal deposition of those bishops whom he wished to remove, and the newcomers examined the fitness of the abbots. The break with the past, however, came more slowly than is often realized. English abbots of unimportant houses persisted for some time. Even in 1087 there were still on the episcopal bench one of Edward's English bishops and two men who had been his clerks. But as William and his sons steadfastly refused to promote Englishmen to high ecclesiastical office, the superstructure became completely foreign, although not exclusively Norman. At the same time, as in the secular sphere, the much larger infra-structure remained almost untouched. The monastic communities were only gradually, and never entirely, normanized. There was almost no interference with the village priests. . . .

Lanfranc[5] held a few legislative councils at the beginning of his rule, in which some common abuses were condemned and the bishops were ordered to reform their dioceses. Archbishop Anselm took up the task again in Henry I's reign, and there was much conciliar activity under Stephen. But the essential feature

[5] The Conqueror appointed Lanfranc archbishop of Canterbury in 1070.

of Anglo-Norman ecclesiastical government was the responsibility of the bishops, under metropolitan guidance, for the government of the church. There was nothing novel in this or in the spiritual charge. Simony (the selling of spiritual offices and services) was no special problem in England; the marriage and sexual immorality of the clergy was a problem everywhere. The drive against the latter sin was set in motion again by enacting the moderate rules of the Norman church against offenders. But, as everything depended on the zeal of the diocesan bishop, the effect was unequal. The most zealous persecutor of the married clergy seems to have been the Englishman, St. Wulfstan of Worcester.

More successful than the moral reform was the reorganization of episcopal administration and justice. The new bishops found that in England they lacked some of the rights which their brethren enjoyed in Normandy. These were granted to them by William. They were to have a monopoly of the ordeals and unfettered spiritual jurisdiction in their dioceses. They quickly appointed their own justiciars and archdeacons and began to withdraw cases, and their profits, from the shire and hundred courts into their own synods and tribunals. No encouragement was given to monastic claims to exemption from episcopal jurisdiction: Lanfranc dealt harshly with St. Augustine's, Canterbury. Nor did most Norman bishops care for the monastic communities which in some dioceses served the cathedral church. But an initial attempt to suppress them was frustrated by English indignation to which Lanfranc and then the pope rallied. Where there were cathedral chapters formed of clerks or canons the bishops began to refashion them on Norman lines.

The new bishops almost immediately began the rebuilding of their cathedral church. They had little initial respect for the English past, pulled down the ancient edifices with their holy associations, and, wealthy, ambitious, determined to impress, began noble structures which, when they have survived, still impress to-day. The remains of English saints, buried in the churches, were often treated roughly. But the disinterments and the question of the translation of the relics, aroused curiosity, for the new masters quite understandably refused to treat as saints men who had no legend. The result was much historical research in the communities and the production of a new corpus of hagiographical writings in Latin, which not only preserved the history of the English church but also helped towards devotional continuity. . . .

The Conquest gave the English church a new look. Externally there was the rebuilding, internally the thorough administrative reorganization and the replacement of the vernacular culture by one more Latin and French in tone. As in secular society, the cleavage between the higher and the lower ranks had been widened. Yet it would be a mistake to think that there was a novel cleavage between the church and the laity. It is true that the reanimated ecclesiastical government gave the church a more distinct appearance and that the purpose of the reformers was to insist on the difference between the two orders; but in social attitudes the Normans were as conservative as the English. The Conqueror, accustomed to ruling the Norman church, exercised the ecclesiastical rights of an English king without hesitation, and may well have extended them. He appointed to bishoprics and royal abbeys; he demanded temporal services from his ecclesiastical vassals; he presided over ecclesiastical councils or licensed their actions. More novel, perhaps, he restricted the church's power to exercise justice over his barons and servants, and closely controlled its intercourse with Rome. In the face of papal schism he ruled that no pope could be recognized in England without royal approval, and, noting the growth of papal interference in domestic affairs, he insisted that all correspondence with Rome should pass through his hands and no papal legate should enter the kingdom without his permission. The English church remained a national church, with the king its effective head.

William rebuffed all novel claims that emanated from the reformed papacy. He would not hold England as a papal fief, he would not allow his archbishops to be ordered about by the pope. Indeed, when Gregory VII lost Rome, the English church seems to have acknowledged no outside superior, a situation which William Rufus was pleased to prolong. . . .

A new power was arising in Christendom to which even English kings and bishops had to give heed. But the development of ecclesiastical institutions and pretensions within the kingdom and the growth of papal interference, both noticeable in Stephen's reign, were hardly in any sense a direct result of the Norman conquest. Two opposing tendencies have to be borne in mind: the union of England and Normandy facilitated the entry of new ideas for which the Normans themselves were not responsible, which, indeed, they often disliked; but the impact of these was delayed by strong Norman kingship, behind which shield most prelates preferred to shelter.

It can hardly be denied that the effects of the Norman conquest were wide and lasting. Had the kingdom remained Anglo-Danish, within a Scandinavian orbit, it would have developed far differently. Nevertheless it is probable that much of the Norman contribution to the English way of life only became significant because there was an Angevin "conquest" in 1154. The Angevins were more truly French than the Normans had been in 1066, if only because in the course of that century French culture had itself become more distinctive. Under the early Angevins the attraction of the French court became so strong that England became almost a French province.

Yet England did not become part of France; and modern Frenchmen regard the English as Anglo-Saxons. One of the reasons for this later withdrawal was the very nature of the society which Norman rule had produced. The Normans in Apulia and Sicily, in England, Scotland, Ireland and the Christian Orient made their own distinctive contribution, but also assumed much of the local colour. They were a possessive race, exploiters, a true aristocracy, organizers, builders, traders, men who lived on others, greedy, but observing some restraint, careful of their lands and tenantry, respectful of local custom. Relatively unprejudiced, they were happy to lord it over any indigenous culture. Without much power of invention, they were both prepared to leave well alone and also quick to grasp the ideas of others and use them to their own advantage.

It is these qualities which make it so difficult to analyse with assurance the exact effects of the Norman conquest. The Normans neither destroyed all things English nor sank entirely into their background. Nor did they have enough time to assimilate all the ingredients and create a homogeneous structure. In 1153 the new kingdom was inchoate, diversified, inconsistent, capable of several different developments. There was increasing denationalization in the highest ranks, a growing insularity among the lesser baronage and the still largely untouched indigenous population beneath, each with its own customs. The Angevins took this strange inheritance in hand and gave it their own impression.

PART THREE

The Problem Of Feudalism:
Its Earlier Phases

1 FROM William Stubbs

The Constitutional History of England

Bishop Stubbs' monumental work, The Constitutional History of
England *[to 1485], first published in three volumes between 1874 and
1878, was described by Sir Frank Stenton as the "foundation of mod-
ern research in this field," but has been condemned unreservedly by
H.G. Richardson and G.O. Sayles in their* Governance of Mediaeval
England *(Edinburgh, 1963): "In the mountain of chaff the wheat is
now of little account, and the chaff is fit only to be thrown away."
Few modern historians would agree with this outright rejection.*

*In the passage quoted below Stubbs addresses himself to the problem
of English feudalism and, in particular, to the question of whether
feudalism was introduced suddenly and completely into England by
the Conqueror and his Normans. Stubbs' views on this matter were
moderate, and, on the whole, his approach tends to be evolutionary
rather than revolutionary.*

It is unnecessary to recapitulate here all the points in which
the Anglo-Saxon institutions were already approaching the feudal
model; it may be assumed that the actual obligation of military
service was much the same in both systems, and that even the
amount of land which was bound to furnish a mounted warrior
was the same, however the conformity may have been produced. . . .

It has, for want of direct and distinct historical statement, been
held that the military tenure, the most prominent feature of
historical feudalism, was itself introduced by the same gradual
process which we have assumed in the case of the feudal usages
in general. We have no light on the point from any original grant
made by the Conqueror to a lay follower; and in the absence

SOURCE. William Stubbs, *The Constitutional History of England*, sixth
edition, Oxford: The Clarendon Press, 1897, Vol. I, pp. 283–287. Reprinted
by permission of the Clarendon Press, Oxford.

of any general enactment we cannot assign the introduction of the system to any direct measure of law. Nor does the exaction of military service involve the immediate carving out of the land into knights' fees. The obligation of national defence was incumbent as of old on all land-owners, and the customary service of one fully armed man for each five hides was probably at the rate at which the newly endowed follower of the king would be expected to discharge his duty. The wording of the Domesday survey does not imply that in this respect the new military service differed from the old: the land is marked out not into knights' fees but into hides, and the number of knights to be furnished by a particular feudatory would be ascertained by inquiring the number of hides that he held, without apportioning the particular acres that were to support the particular knight. On the other hand, the early date at which the due service (debitum servitium) of feudal tenants appears as fixed, goes a long way to prove that it was settled in each case at the time of the royal grant.

It must not however be assumed that this process was other than gradual. Our earliest information is derived from the notices of ecclesiastical practice. Lanfranc, we are told, turned the drengs, the rent-paying tenants of his archiepiscopal estates, into knights for the defence of the country: he enfeoffed a certain number of knights who performed the military service due from the archiepiscopal barony. This had been done before the Domesday survey, and almost necessarily implies that a like measure had been taken by the lay vassals. Lanfranc likewise maintained ten knights to answer for the military service due from the convent of Christ Church, which made over to him, in consideration of the relief, land worth two hundred pounds annually. The value of the knight's fee must already have been fixed at twenty pounds a year. In the reign of William Rufus the abbot of Ramsey obtained a charter which exempted his monastery from the service of ten knights due from it on festivals, substituting the obligation to furnish three knights to perform service on the north of the Thames: a proof that the lands of that house had not yet been divided into knights' fees. In the next reign we may infer from the favour granted by the king to the knights who defend their lands "per loricas," that is, by the hauberk, that their demesne lands shall be exempt from pecuniary taxation, that the process of definite military infeudation had largely advanced. But it was not even yet forced on the clerical or monastic estates. When in 1167[1] the abbot of Milton in Dorset was questioned as to the number of knights' fees for which he had to account, he replied that all the services due from his monastery were discharged out of the demesne; but he added that in the reign of Henry I, during a vacancy in the abbacy, bishop Roger of Salisbury had enfeoffed two knights out of the abbey lands, he had however subsequently reversed the act and had restored the lands whose tenure had been thus altered to their original condition of rent-paying estate or socage. The very term "the new feoffment," which was applied to the knights' fees created between the death of Henry I and the year in which the account preserved in the Black Book of the Exchequer was taken, proves that the process was going on for nearly a hundred years, and that the form in which the knights' fees appear when called on by Henry II for scutage[2] was most probably the result of a series of compositions by which the great vassals relieved their lands from a general burden by carving out particular estates the holders of which performed the services due from the whole; it was a matter of convenience and not of tyrannical pressure. The statement of Ordericus Vitalis that the Conqueror "distributed lands to his knights in such fashion that the kingdom of England should have for ever 60,000 knights, and furnish them at the king's command according to the occasion," must be regarded as one of the many numerical exaggerations of the early historians. The officers of the Exchequer in the twelfth century were quite unable to fix the number of existing knights' fees.

[1] Actually 1166, in Henry II's great survey of knightly enfeoffments, the returns of which are known as the *Cartae Baronum*.

[2] Scutage is the payment of money to one's lord in lieu of military service.

2 FROM   *Edward A. Freeman*
The History of the Norman Conquest

The passage below summarizes Freeman's gradualist views on the development of feudalism in England.

It shows how utterly the history of law has been misunderstood by those whose special business it is to understand it, when we see lawyer after lawyer telling the world that William the Conqueror introduced the "Feudal System" into England. Ingenious writers have looked on that great Gemót[1] of Salisbury which was held in the year before William's death as the actual moment when this amazing revolution took place. That is to say, they have picked out, as the act by which a Feudal System was introduced in England, the very act by which William's far-seeing wisdom took care that no Feudal System ever should grow up in England. So far as any Feudal System ever existed anywhere, its principle was that every tenant-in-chief of the Crown should make himself as nearly a sovereign prince as he could, that his under-tenants should owe allegiance and obedience to their immedaite lord only, and not to the royal or Imperial head. The principle of William's legislation was that every man throughout the realm of England should plight his allegiance to his lord the King, and should pay obedience to the laws which were decreed by his lord the King and his Witan. Instead of William introducing a Feudal System into England, instead of consenting to sink from the

[1] Assembly.

SOURCE. Edward A. Freeman, *The History of the Norman Conquest of England*, second edition, Oxford: The Clarendon Press, 1870–1879, Vol. V, pp. 366–373 and 376–378. Reprinted by permission of the Clarendon Press, Oxford.

national King of the whole nation into the personal lord of a few men in the nation, he stopped for ever any tendencies— whether tendencies at work before his coming or tendencies brought in by the circumstances of his coming—which could lower the King of the English to the level of the feudal Kings of the mainland. The tendency of feudalism is to a divided land, with a weak central government, or no central government at all. Every such tendency William checked, while he strengthened every tendency which could help him in establishing a strong central government over an united realm. To that end he pre- served the ancient laws and institutions, laws and institutions which he had no temptation to sweep away, because they could be easily turned into the best instruments for compassing his object. Under the forms of lawful succession, he reigned as a conqueror; under the forms of free institutions, he reigned as a despot. In truth the acts of the despot were needed to undo the acts of the conqueror. As conqueror, he brought us to the brink of feudal anarchy; as despot, he saved us from passing the brink. Of any Feudal System, looked on as a form of government, or rather of no-government, William, instead of being the introducer, was the mightiest and most successful enemy.

But the words *feudal* and *feudalism* have, in practice at least, two distinct meanings. The so-called Feudal System, that is, the break up of all national unity in a kingdom, undoubtedly grew out of the feudal tenure of land. But the feudal tenure of land does not in itself imply any weakness on the part of the central power. Even if we look merely to the tenure of land, it would be quite untrue to say that William introduced feudalism into England. For, on the one hand, William did not systematically introduce any new kind of tenures; and, on the other hand, tendencies in a feudal direction had been busily at work long before his coming. Here again the Conquest merely hastened and completed changes which had already begun. The essence of a feudal tenure is the holding of land by the grant of a lord, instead of holding it simply as a member of the commonwealth. The holder of a primitive *eðel*[2] held his land of no man; he had no lord; as a member of the com- monwealth, he owed to the King or other chief of the common-

---

[2] Free holding.

wealth such obedience as the law prescribed, but the tie was purely political and not personal. But the man who received a grant of land on condition of any service, military or otherwise, stood to his lord in a relation which was not only political but personal. If to this tenure an act of personal commendation was added, the full feudal relation was created. . . . Things in England, as in other parts of Western Europe, were fast tending in a feudal direction before William came into England. His coming gave those tendencies a greatly increased strength. He and his followers came from lands where feudal ideas had made far swifter advances than in England. To the mass of his followers a feudal tenure, a military tenure, must have seemed the natural and universal way of holding land. A primitive *eðel*, even a grant of bookland[3] not charged with any particular services, must have seemed to them something strange and unintelligible. Even to the keen eye of William himself they may well have seemed strange, though assuredly they did not seem unintelligible. And the great facts of William's reign did everything to strengthen the doctrine that land should be held of a lord. We have seen that, from the beginning, he dealt with all lay estates in England as land forfeited to the Crown, which the King granted out afresh, whether the grant was to the former owner or to some new grantee. The foreign soldier who received his reward in a grant of English land held that land, as a plain matter of fact and without any legal subtleties, as a personal gift from King William. The Englishman who bought back his land, or received it back again as alms, did not hold it as a gift in exactly the same sense as his Norman neighbour, but it was a royal grant by something more than a mere legal fiction. His land had been, if only for a moment, in the King's hands to be dealt with as the King chose; and the King had chosen to give it back to him, rather than to keep it himself or to give it to anybody else. The lawyers' doctrine that all land must be a grant from the Crown is thus accidentally an historical truth. It became true by virtue of a single act of William's reign, which no law-book records, and which most likely no lawyer ever thought of. In this way William became systematically to every landowner in his realm, what earlier Kings had incidentally

---

[3] Land granted by charter.

been to many of them, a personal grantor as well as a political chief. There was no longer such a thing as an eðel; all was bookland, bookland too held only by the actual gift of the reigning King or by his confirmation of some earlier gift. And the act of personal homage, the commendation of a man to his lord, an act which, though not implied in the grant of land, no doubt always accompanied it, brought every grantee into a strictly feudal relation to his sovereign. The King's Thegns[4] became the King's tenants-in-chief. They had been his tenants-in-chief before; they remained his Thegns still, but now the one name gradually displaced the other, not merely because the one name was English and the other name French, but because the leading ideas conveyed by the two names now changed places. From henceforth the idea of personal commendation implied in the word Thegn became of less importance than the idea of the tenure of land implied in the name tenant-in-chief. The effect of William's confiscations and grants was to bring the tenure of land, the holding of land as a grant from a lord, into a prominence which it had never held before, to make it in short the chief element in the polity of the kingdom. In this way the same reign which most effectually hindered the growth of feudalism in its political aspect, most effectually strengthened feudalism as a form of the tenure of land. And, in so doing, it strengthened thereby all those peculiar social relations and ideas which gather round such a tenure. As the old Eorls died out before the Thegns, so the Thegns died out before the new names of knight and gentleman.

The circumstances of the reign of William thus gave a great impulse to one aspect of feudal ideas; but it does not appear that he made any direct innovations in the law with regard to the tenure of land. Nothing is more certain than that, from one end of Domesday to the other, there is not a trace of military tenures as they were afterwards understood. As I have had to point out over and over again, the grantee of William, whether the old owner or a new one, held his land as it had been held in the days of King Edward. The Value of the land might have risen or fallen, and its taxation might have risen or fallen in proportion; but the Survey gives no sign that any land had been made sub-

---

[4] The chief lay landholders in pre-Conquest England.

ject to any burthens of a different kind from those which it had borne in earlier times. That the word *feudum* or *fief* is constantly used proves nothing; it accurately described the holding of all land since the general redemption, as it would have accurately described the holding of much land before William's coming. Nor is anything proved by the constant occurrence, not indeed in name but in fact, of that which was afterwards known as *subinfeudation*. It was in the nature of things that the grantee of a great estate should grant out parts of it again to smaller owners, who would, whatever was their tenure, become his men. In every page of Domesday we hear of the "men" of this or that great land-owner, and the practice of commendation is referred to almost as commonly. Still we hear of nothing in Domesday which can be called knight-service or military tenure in the later sense. The old obligations remain. The primæval duty of military service, due, not to a lord as a lord, but to the state and to the King as its head, went on under King William as it had gone on under King Edward. . . .

There is no ground then for thinking that William directly or systematically introduced any new kind of tenure into the holding of English lands. There is nothing to suggest any such belief, either in the Chronicles of his reign, in the Survey which is his greatest monument, in the genuine, or even in the spurious, remains of his legislation. . . . But, when we come to the reign next but one, we are met by a document which shows us that, within thirteen years after the Conqueror's death, not only the military tenures, but the worst abuses of the military tenures, were in full force in England. The great charter of Henry the First,[5] the groundwork of the greater charter of John, and thereby the groundwork of all later English legislation, is filled with promises to abolish the very same class of abuses which were at last swept away by the famous statute of Charles the Second. In that charter the military tenures are taken for granted. What is provided against is their being perverted, as they had been in the days of Rufus, into engines of oppression. It is assumed that the King lays certain feudal burthens on his tenants-in-chief; it is assumed that these tenants-in-chief lay burthens of the same

[5] A. D. 1100.

kind on their under-tenants. The object of the charter is not to abolish the rights of either the higher or the lower lord, but only to insure that those rights should be used with some degree of moderation. The lord's right of marriage, of wardship, of relief, the rights under which Englishmen groaned down to the days of our last civil war, are all taken for granted; the yoke is simply to be lightened in practice. . . . Its promises and its decrees strike at the worst evils of the military tenures as they existed in England for ages afterwards; they are an instance of enlightened and beneficent legislation, which was hindered, either by lack of power or lack of will, from being fully or lastingly carried into effect. But they are none the less a witness, telling us that those same points in the military tenures which were felt as grievances in after times were felt as grievances when the military tenures were themselves something new. And they are none the less a witness to the fact that the military tenures had been fully established and wrought into a systematic shape before the accession of Henry. There is no surer witness to the firm establishment of an institution than that it is thought possible to reform its abuses without abolishing the institution itself. But we have seen that in the days of the Conqueror there was no such elaborate system of tenures, carrying with it such well-defined consequences, as appears in the state of things which the charter of Henry was meant to reform. The inference is obvious. The system of military tenures, and the oppressive consequences which were held to flow from them, were a work of the days of William Rufus.

When we have got thus far, we can hardly fail to follow the lead of the greatest scholar of our times[6] in marking the creation of this new and oppressive system, at all events the putting of it into a legal and formal shape, as the work of a single well-known man. We can feel little doubt in saying that the man who organized the system of feudal oppression was that same Randolf Flambard[7] whom we have met with as the author of so much evil, and whom a contemporary writer does not scruple to speak

---

[6] Stubbs.

[7] Flambard served as chief minister under King William Rufus and was appointed bishop of Durham late in the reign.

of as the dregs of wickedness. The argument seems complete. Flambard is distinctly charged with being the author of certain new and evil customs with regard to spiritual holdings; it follows, almost as a matter of course, that he was the author of the exactly analogous and equally oppressive changes which were brought in at the same time with regard to lay holdings.

If then there was any time when "the Feudal System" could be said to be introduced into England, it was assuredly, not in the days of William the Conqueror, but in the days of William the Red. It would be more accurate to say that, all that we are really concerned with, that is, not an imaginary "Feudal System," but a system of feudal land-tenures, was not introduced into England at all, but was devised on English ground by the malignant genius of the minister of Rufus. Tendencies which had been at work before the Conquest, and to which the Conquest gave increased strength, were by him pushed to their logical results, and were worked into an harmonious system of oppression.

3   FROM   *John Horace Round*
"The Introduction of Knight Service into England"

This is the classical statement of the "feudal revolution" hypothesis with which Round startled the English scholarly world of the 1890's.

"The growth of knighthood is a subject on which the greatest obscurity prevails; and the most probable explanation of its existence in England, the theory that it is a translation into Norman forms of the thegnage of the Anglo-Saxon law, can only be stated as probable."—STUBBS, *Const. Hist.*, i. 260.

In approaching the consideration of the institutional changes and modifications of polity resulting from the Norman Conquest,

SOURCE. John Horace Round, *Feudal England*, London: Sonnenschein & Company, 1895, pp. 225–231, 234, 246–251, 261 and 303–305.

the most conspicuous phenomenon to attract attention is undoubtedly the introduction of what it is convenient to term the feudal system. In the present paper I propose to discuss one branch only of that process, namely, the introduction of that military tenure which Dr. Stubbs has termed "the most prominent feature of historical feudalism."

In accordance with the anticataclysmic tendencies of modern thought, the most recent students of this obscure problem have agreed to adopt the theory of gradual development and growth. The old views on the subject are discredited as crude and unhistorical: they are replaced by confident enunciation of the theory to which I have referred. But when we examine the matter closely, when we ask for details of the process by which the Anglo-Saxon thegn developed into the Norman knight, we are met at once by the frank confession that "between the picture drawn in Domesday and the state of affairs which the charter of Henry I was designed to remedy, there is a difference which the short interval of time will not account for." To meet this difficulty, to account for this flaw in the unbroken continuity of the series, a *Deus ex machina* has been found in the person of Ranulf Flambard.

Now this solution of the difficulty will scarcely, I venture to think, bear the test of investigation. It appears to have originated in Dr. Stubbs' suggestion that there must have been, between the days of Henry I and of William I, "some skilful organising hand working with neither justice nor mercy—a suggestion subsequently amplified into the statement that it is to Ranulf Flambard "without doubt that the systematic organisation of the exactions" under William Rufus "is to be attributed," and that by him "the royal chains were unrelentingly pressed," his policy being "to tighten as much as possible the hold which the feudal law gave to the king on all feudatories temporal and spiritual." There is nothing here that can be called in question, but there is also nothing, be it observed, to prove that either "feudal law" or "military tenure" was introduced by Ranulf Flambard. Indeed, with his usual caution and unfailing sound judgment, our great historian is careful to admit that "it is not quite so clear" in the case of the lay as of the church fiefs "that all the evil customs owed their origin to the reign of William Rufus." And, even if they did, they were, it must be remembered, distinctly abuses —"evil customs," as Henry I himself terms them in his charter— namely (in the matter we are considering), "*excessive* exactions in the way of reliefs, marriages and wardships, debts to the crown, and forfeiture. In the place," we are told, "of *unlimited* demands on these heads, the charter promises, not indeed fixed amercements, but a return to ancient equitable custom." All this refers, it will be seen, to the abuse of an existing institution, not to the introduction of a new one. The fact is that Ranulf's proceedings have been assigned a quite exceptional and undue importance. Broadly speaking, his actions fall under a law too often lost sight of, namely, that when the crown was strong it pressed, through the official bureaucracy, its claims to the uttermost; and when it found itself weak, it renounced them so far as it was compelled. Take, for instance, this very charter issued by Henry I, when he was "playing to the gallery," and seeking general support: what was the value of its promises? They were broken, says Mr. Freeman, to the Church; they were probably broken, says Dr. Stubbs, to the knights; and they were certainly broken, I may add, to the unfortunate tenants-in-chief, whom the Pipe-Roll of 1130 shows us suffering from those same excessive exactions, of which the monopoly is assigned to Ranulf Flambard, and which "the Lion of Justice"[1] had so virtuously renounced. I might similarly adduce the exactions from the Church by that excellent king, Henry II (1159) . . . but it is needless to multiply examples of the struggle between the interests of the crown and those of its tenants-in-chief, which was as fierce as ever when, in later days, it led to the provisions of the Great Charter. What the barons, lay and spiritual, complained of from first to last, was not the feudal system that accompanied their military tenure, but the abuse of that system in the excessive demands of the crown.

Mr. Freeman, however, who had an equal horror of Ranulf Flambard and of the "feudal system," did not hesitate to connect the two more closely even than Dr. Stubbs, though invoking the authority of the latter in support of his extreme views. . . .

As the writer's line of argument is avowedly that of Dr.

---

[1] A nickname of Henry I.

Stubbs, it is only necessary to consider the point of difference between them. Where his predecessor saw in Henry's charter the proof that Ranulf Flambard had abused the existing feudal system by "excessive" and "unlimited" demands, Mr. Freeman held, and endeavoured to convince us, that he had introduced not merely abuses of the system, but the actual system itself. The question virtually turns on the first clause of the charter; and it will not, I think, be doubted that Dr. Stubbs is right in adopting its natural meaning, namely, that the novelty introduced by Ranulf was not the *relevatio* itself, but its abuse in "excessive exactions." Indeed, even Mr. Freeman had virtually to admit the point. If, then, the argument breaks down, if Ranulf cannot be shown to have "devised" military tenure, how are we to bridge over the alleged chasm between the date of Domesday (1086) and that of Henry's charter (1100)? The answer is simply that the difficulty is created by the very theory I am discussing: it is based on the assumption that William I did not introduce military tenure, combined with the fact that "within thirteen years after the Conqueror's death, not only the military tenures, but the worst abuses of the military tenures, were in full force in England." But, here again, when we examine the evidence, we find that this assumption is based on the silence, or alleged silence, of Domesday Book. Now no one was better aware than Mr. Freeman, as an ardent student of "the great Record," that to argue from the silence of Domesday is an error as dangerous as it is common. Speaking from a rather wide acquaintance with topographical works, I know of no pitfall into which the local antiquary is more liable to fall. Wonderful are the things that people look for in the pages of the great survey; I am always reminded of Mr. Secretary Pepys' writing for information as to what it contained "concerning the sea and the dominion thereof." Like other inquests, the Domesday Survey—"the great inquest of all," as Dr. Stubbs terms it—was intended for a special purpose; special questions were asked, and these questions were answered in the returns. So with the "Inquest of Sheriffs" in 1170; so also with the Inquest of Knights, if I may so term it, in 1166. In each case the questions asked are, practically, known to us, and in each they are entirely different. Therefore, when Mr. Freeman writes—

"The survey nowhere employs the feudal language which became familiar in the twelfth century. Compare, for instance, the records in the first volume of Hearne's *Liber Niger Scaccarii*.[2] In this last we find something about knights' fees in every page. In Domesday there is not a word—"

it is in no spirit of captious criticism, but from the necessity of demolishing the argument, that I liken it to basing conclusions on the fact that in the census returns we find something about population in every page, while in the return of owners of land there is not a word. As the inquest of 1166 sought solely for information on knights and their fees, the returns to it naturally contain "something about knights' fees in every page"; on the other hand, "the payment or non-payment of the *geld* is a matter which appears in every page of the survey" [of 1086] because "the formal immediate cause of taking the survey was to secure its full and fair assessment." Nor is this all. When the writer asserts that "in Domesday there is not a word" about knights' fees, he greatly overstates his case, as indeed is shown by the passages he proceeds to quote. I shall be able to prove, further on, that knights' fees existed in cases where Domesday does not mention them, but even the incidental notices found in the Great Survey are quite sufficient to disprove its alleged silence on the subject. As Mr. Freeman has well observed:—

"Its most incidental notices are sometimes the most precious. We have seen that it is to an incidental, an almost accidental notice in the Survey that we owe our knowledge of the great fact of the general redemption of lands."

Here then the writer does not hesitate to base on a single accidental notice the existence of an event quite as widespread and important as the introduction of knight service.

I have now endeavoured to make plain one of the chief flaws in the view at present accepted, namely, that it is mainly grounded on the negative evidence of Domesday, which evidence will not

---

[2] *Black Book of the Exchequer.*

bear the construction that has been placed upon it,—and further that, even if it did, we should be landed in a fresh difficulty, the gulf between Domesday and Henry's charter being only to be bridged by the assumption that Ranulf Flambard "devised" and introduced military tenure, with its results—an assumption, we have seen, which the facts of the case not only fail to support, but even discountenance wholly.

Let us pass to a second difficulty. When we ask the advocates of the view I am discussing what determined the number of knights due to the crown from a tenant-in-chief, we obtain, I venture to assert, no definite answer. At times we are told that it was the number of his hides; at times that it was the value of his estate. . . .

[The opinions of several of Round's contemporaries are here set forth.]

Mr. Freeman's views need not detain us, for he unhesitatingly accepts Dr. Stubbs' arguments as proving that the Norman military tenure was based on "the old service of a man from each five hides of land."

We find then, I submit, that the recognised leaders of existing opinion on the subject cannot agree among themselves in giving us a clear answer, when we ask them what determined the amount of "service" due from a Norman tenant-in-chief, or, in other words, how that "service" was developed in unbroken continuity from Anglo-Saxon obligations.

The third point that I would raise is this. Even assuming that the amount of "service" bore a fixed proportion—whether in pecuniary or territorial units—to the extent of possession, we are, surely, at once confronted by the difficulty that the owner of x units of possession would be compelled, for the discharge of his military obligations, to enfeoff x knights, assigning a "unit" to each. A tenant-in-chief, to take a concrete instance, whose fief was worth £100 a year, would have to provide *ex hypothesi* five knights; if, as was quite usual, he enfeoffed the full number, he would have to assign to each knight twenty librates of land (which I may at once, though anticipating, admit was the normal value of a knight's fee), that is to say, the crown would have forestalled Henry George, and the luckless *baro* would see the entire value of his estate swallowed up in the discharge of its obligations. What his position would be in cases where, as often, he enfeoffed more knights than he required, arithmetic is unable to determine. I cannot understand how this obvious difficulty has been so strangely overlooked. . . .

The essential feature we have to keep in view when examining the growth of knight-service is the *servitium debitum*, or quota of knight-service due to the crown from each fief.

This has, I venture to think, been obscured and lost sight of in the generalizations and vague writing about the "gradual process" of development. It is difficult for me to traverse the arguments of Gneist, Stubbs and Freeman, because we consider the subject from such wholly different standpoints. For them the introduction of knight-service means the process of subinfeudation on the several fiefs; for me it means the grant of fiefs to be held from the crown by knight service. Thus the process which absorbs the attention of the school whose views I am opposing is for me a matter of mere secondary importance. The whole question turns upon the point whether or not the tenants-in-chief received their fiefs to hold of the crown by a quota of military service, or not. If they did, it would depend simply on their individual inclinations, whether, or how far, they had recourse to subinfeudation. It was not a matter of principle at all; it was, as Dr. Stubbs himself puts it, "a matter of convenience," a mere detail. What we have to consider is not the relation between the tenant-in-chief and his under-tenants, but that between the king and his tenants-in-chief: for this was the primary relation that determined all below it.

The assumption that the Conqueror cannot have introduced any new principle in the tenure of land lies at the root of the matter. Assuming this, one must of course seek elsewhere for the introduction of knight service. Have not the difficulties of the accepted view arisen from its exponents approaching the problem from the wrong point of view? The tendency to exalt the English and depreciate the Norman element in our constitutional development has led them I think, and especially Mr. Freeman, to seek in Anglo-Saxon institutions an explanation of feudal phenomena. This tendency is manifest in their conclusions on the great council: it colours no less strongly their views on knight-service. In neither case can they bring themselves to adopt the feudal standpoint or to enter into the feudal spirit. It is to this that I attribute their disposition to bring the crown face to face with the under-tenant—or "landowner" as they would prefer to term him—and so to ignore, or at least to minimise the importance of the tenant-in-chief, the "middleman" of the feudal system. Making every allowance for the policy of the Conqueror in insisting on the direct allegiance of the under-tenant to the crown, and thereby checking the disintegrating influence of a perfect feudal system, the fact remains what we may term the "military service" bargain was a bargain between the crown and the tenant-in-chief, not between, the crown and his under-tenants. It follows from this that so long as the "baron" (or "tenant-in-chief") discharged his *servitium debitum* to the crown, the king had no right to look beyond the "baron," who was himself and alone responsible for the discharge of this service. It is, indeed, in this responsibility that lies the key to the situation. If the under-tenant of a knight's fee failed to discharge his service, it was not to him, but to his lord, that the crown betook itself. "I know nothing of your tenant," was in effect the king's position; "you owe me, for the tenure of your fief, the service of so many knights, and that service must be performed, whether your under-tenants repudiate their obligations to yourself or not." . . .

Let us then apply ourselves directly to the quotas of military service due from the "barons" to the crown, and see if, when ascertained, they throw any fresh light on the real problem: . . .

I shall analyse the church fiefs first, because we can ascertain, virtually with exactitude, the *servitium debitum* of every prelate and of every head of a religious house who held by knight-service. The importance of these figures, together with the fact that they have never, so far as I know, been set forth till now, has induced me to append them here in full detail.[3]

[3] The following figures are derived from the *Cartae Baronum* of 1166 and the scutage accounts of Henry II's reign.

SEE	SERVICE DUE Knights		SEE	SERVICE DUE Knights
Canterbury	60		Bath	20
Winchester	60		London	20
Lincoln	60		Exeter	17½
Worcester	50 [60]		"Chester"	15
Norwich	40		Hereford	15
Ely	40		Durham	10
Salisbury	32		Chichester	4 [2]
York	20 [7]			

Every English see then in existence is thus accounted for with the solitary and significant exceptions of Carlisle and Rochester. The latter see, we know, had enfeoffed knights, for their names are recorded *(tempt.* Hen. I, I think, from internal evidence) are recorded in the *Textus Roffensis* (p. 223); the former had been created after the date when, as I shall argue, the Conqueror fixed the knight-service due from the fees.

In the above list the figures in brackets refer to the assessments previous to 1166. Three changes were made at, or about, that date. The Bishop of Worcester, in accordance with the protest he had made from the beginning of the reign, obtained a reduction of his quota from sixty knights to fifty; while the Archbishop of York's *servitium* was raised from seven knights to twenty, and that of the Bishop of Chichester from two knights to four. . . .

[Round next provides quotas of monasteries and lay fiefs.]

I am anxious to make absolutely clear the point that between the accepted view and the view which I advance, no compromise is possible. The two are radically opposed. As against the theory that the military obligation of the Anglo-Norman tenant-in-chief was determined by the assessment of his holding, whether in hidage or in value, I maintain that the extent of that obligation was not determined by his holding, but was fixed in relation to, and expressed in terms of, the *constabularia* of ten knights, the unit of the feudal host. And I, consequently, hold that his military service was in no way derived or developed from that of the Anglo-Saxons, but was arbitrarily fixed by the king, from

whom he received his fief, irrespective both of its size and of all
pre-existent arrangements. . . .

I propose to quote as a climax to my argument the writ printed
below. Startling as it may read, for its early date, to the holders
of the accepted view, the vigour of its language convinced me,
when I found it, that in it King William speaks; nor was there
anything to be gained by forging a document which admits,
by placing on record, the abbey's full liability.

"W. Rex Anglor[um] Attew' abbati de Euesh[am] sal[u]tem.
Precipio tibi quod submoneas omnes illos qui sub ballia et i[us]titia
s[un]t quatin[us] omnes milites quo mihi debent p[ar]atos
h[abe]ant ante me ad octavas pentecostes ap[ud] clarendun[am].
Tu etiam illo die ad me venias et illos quinque milites quos de
abb[at]ia tua mihi debes tec[um] paratos adducas. Teste Eudone
dapif[er]o Ap[ud] Wintoniam."[4]

Being addressed to Æthelwig, the writ, of course, must be
previous to his death in 1077, but I think that we can date it,
perhaps, with precision, and that it belongs to the year 1072. In
that year, says the Ely chronicler, the Conqueror, projecting his
invasion to Scotland,. "jusserat tam abbatibus quam episcopis
totius Angliae debita militiae obsequia transmitti,"[5] a phrase which
applies exactly to the writ before us. In that year, moreover, the
movements of William fit in fairly with the date for which the
feudal levy was here summoned. We know that he visited Normandy in the spring, and invaded Scotland in the summer, and
he might well summon his baronage to meet him on 3rd June,
on his way from Normandy to Scotland, at so convenient a point
as Clarendon. The writ, again, being witnessed at Winchester,
may well have been issued by the king on his way out or back.

---

[4] "William, King of the English, to Æthelwig, abbot of Evesham, greet-
ing. I command that you summon all those who are under your administration and jurisdiction that they bring before me on the Octave of Pentecost
at Clarendon all the knights that they owe me, properly equipped. You, too,
on that day, shall come to me and bring with you, properly equipped, those
five knights which you owe me from your abbacy. Witness Eudo the Stew-
ard. At Winchester."

[5] "ordered the abbots and bishops of all England to send their quotas of
military service."

The direction to the abbot to summon similarly all those beneath his sway who owed military service is probably explained by the special position he occupied as "chief ruler" of several counties at the time. . . . The number of knights which constituted the *servitium debitum* of Evesham was five then as it was afterwards, and this number, as we now know, had been fixed *pro voluntate sua*,[6] in 1070, by the Conqueror.

4   *The Abbot of Evesham's Entry in the Cartae Baronum (1166)*

In the important writ of military summons of about 1072 which Round quotes, the knightly quota of Evesham is given as five men. Nearly a century later—in 1166—this same figure of five knights turns up in the statement prepared by the abbot of Evesham in response to a national survey of knightly enfeoffments of English tenants-in-chief ordered by King Henry II.

Knights' service from Evesham Abbey:
Ranulf "de Coctone" performs the full service of one knight with horses and arms, and the abbot shall pay his expenses so long as he is in the king's service.
Ranulf "de Kinewartone" the same.
Richard of Weston and Richard "de Piplumtone" the same.
Bertram and Payn Travers the same.

[6] "at his own pleasure." Round is referring to a passage from the *Historia Anglorum* of the thirteenth-century St. Albans' chronicler, Matthew Paris, in which, under the year 1070, William I is described as establishing "at his own pleasure" military quotas on the bishoprics and abbeys of England. The report is hardly contemporary with the event, but Round believes that it is verified by much earlier evidence such as the writ above.

SOURCE. "Carta of the Abbey of Evesham," in *The Red Book of the Exchequer*, Hubert Hall, ed., Rolls Series, No. 99, 1896, Vol. I, pp. 301-302.

William of Beauchamp half the service of a knight at the abbot's expense.

The aforesaid are of the old enfeoffment [enfeoffed A.D. 1135 or before].

Richard, son of Maurice of Amberley, half the service of a knight at the abbot's expense, and he alone is of the new enfeoffment [i.e., enfeoffed between 1135 and 1166].

5 FROM *Sir Frank Stenton*

The First Century of English Feudalism: (1066–1166)

Sir Frank Stenton, one of England's most distinguished medievalists of the early and middle years of the twentieth century, presents here further cogent arguments for the Round hypothesis of the Norman introduction of knights' service. Stenton's mood, however, is far more serene and objective than Round's. The important book from which these excerpts have been drawn was published originally in 1932, and was itself based on the Ford Lectures which Stenton delivered at Oxford in 1929.

Within a generation after the battle, the Norman conquerors had established in central and southern England, and introduced into the region beyond Humber, a system of military service which at every point ignored Old English precedent. It is now nearly seventy years since Round traced the history of English knight service back to the unrecorded bargains by which the Conqueror fixed the number of knights due for his service from each of his greater followers. The materials for the study of English feudalism have greatly increased since 1891. Cartularies have been published, Domesday Book has been analysed, the out-

SOURCE Sir Frank Stenton, *The First Century of English Feudalism: 1066–1166*, second edition, Oxford: The Clarendon Press, 1961, pp. 122–129 and 216–217. Reprinted by permission of the Clarendon Press, Oxford.

lines of the feudalism which the Normans knew in their own land have been established. This work has only confirmed Round's main position that the amount of knight service which King William demanded from his several tenants in chief bore no definite relation to the extent or value of their lands. It has also confirmed his more general argument that the feudal society which underlies English life in the centuries after the Conquest represents a definite break away from Old English tradition. The break, indeed, is far from absolute. The relationship between lord and man created by the tie of homage was common to the whole Germanic world. But the development of this relationship had been arrested in England, and only the most tentative of approaches had been made before the Conquest towards the great feudal principle of dependent tenure in return for definite service.

Here and there experiments which seem to tend in this direction have been noted by different scholars. In particular, evidence of a nascent feudalism in tenth-century England has been sought in the famous documents by which Bishop Oswald of Worcester granted out on leases for three lives a considerable proportion of the ancient estates of his church in Worcestershire, Gloucestershire, and Warwickshire. These leases, which in themselves give less information than many other documents of their class, become important when they are read in connexion with a memorandum, addressed by the bishop to King Edgar, and setting out the terms on which he has been granting land to his men. According to this memorandum those who have taken land from the bishop were subject to a great variety of duties. They were bound "to fulfill the law of riding as riding men should," to pay whatever was due to the church of Worcester, namely church-scot, toll, payment for swine-pasture, and "the other dues of the church," and to swear that they would continue in humble subjection to the bishop's commands. They were also bound to apply themselves to supply the bishop's needs, to lend horses, ride themselves, and apparently, though here the bishop is obscure, to burn lime for the work of the church and for bridge-building. The memorandum goes on to state that they were to make the bishop's deer-hedge when he wished to hunt, and it sums up their relationship to their lord in the general statements that they were liable to many other demands in the bishop's name both in respect of the king's service and his own, and that they were always to be subject to the bishop's lordship in respect of the loans which they had received from him and according to their amount. Failure to observe these conditions was to be punished by a money fine or by forfeiture of the holding, and on the expiry of the last of the three lives for which the lease was granted the bishop reserved the right of taking back the land into his own hand or of granting it out again. Whatever general interpretation may be given to this document, it is certainly a deliberate attempt to define the terms under which a great lord has been granting land to his men, and as such it is unique among Old English records.

But between these services and those which were imposed by enfeoffments of the eleventh and twelfth centuries there are two essential differences. The services for which Oswald stipulated were miscellaneous, and he left their exact nature vague. There is no trace in his memorandum of the feudal ideas that the services to be rendered for a tenement should admit of a close definition, and that if more than a single form of service is required from the same holding, the services with which it is associated should be of a cognate character. The services set out by Oswald form a very incoherent series of obligations. They range from hunting service to bridge-building, and at many points resemble the miscellaneous duties of the eleventh-century *geneat*, which are described in the *Rectitudines Singularum Personarum*[1] as "varying according to what is the rule on the estate." It is more significant that Oswald made no attempts to define any of these duties. At every critical point in the memorandum its language shades off into vague assertions of general obligation. It is not the memorandum itself, but a comparison of it and other evidence, which shows that the famous "law of riding" meant not military service, but the duty of escorting a lord from place to

---

[1] The Anglo-Saxon *geneat* occupied an intermediate social position between common peasant and thegn. The *Rectitudines Singularum Personarum* or "Rights and Ranks of People" is a pre-Conquest eleventh-century document describing the obligations of various ranks of peasants to their lord.

place. This vagueness was due to the circumstances under which the memorandum was written. It was not intended as a precise formulation of rights and duties like a later feudal custumal. It was a retrospective document, drawn up to cover a number of grants already made in still more general terms. Already before the earliest date at which it can have been composed, Oswald had been granting leases to his men, and each of these leases must have been governed by its own set of implicit understandings. Oswald was clearly endeavouring to indicate in outline the relationship which he expected all who held loan-land of him to observe towards him and his church. A document written for such a purpose was not the place for exact definitions. But there can have been no real movement towards any conceptions which can properly be called feudal in a society where such a relationship needed to be clarified in such a way. . . .

It might be expected that a record drawn up under these conditions would say something definite about the military service due from the bishop's tenants. There can be no doubt that many of them were bound by their social position to serve in war. Most of the men to whom Oswald is known to have granted leases seem to have been thegns. . . .

If need arose, such men would certainly be required to serve in the host with others of their class, and a passage in Hemming's cartulary which speaks of the *ductor exercitus episcopi ad servitium regis*[2] suggests that they would come under the command of an officer responsible to the bishop. It is therefore important to observe that neither the memorandum nor the leases which it helps to interpret ever imply that the bishop has given land to a tenant in order that he may do military service. The bishop no doubt expected his tenant to see that the men on the estate did the fyrd-service due by custom from its peasantry, but neither memorandum nor leases ever refer to the military service of the lessee as distinct from that of the peasants under him. If one of Oswald's tenants is of thegnly rank, he will serve because service is expected from a man of his class by a custom indistinguishable from law. If he fails in this service, he must answer for it to the bishop, and the bishop to the king, but his service

2 "Leader of the bishop's army in the king's service."

is a matter of personal duty, irrespective of the terms on which he has received land from his lord. None of all the documents which have come from Bishop Oswald offers any anticipation of the feudal principle by which a man will take land from a lord in return for a definite amount of military service to be rendered in respect of his tenure. . . .

. . . A few words may be said on one general question . . . the question whether anything that should be called feudalism had existed in England before the Norman Conquest. The question will never be finally answered, for feudalism is only a term invented for the historian's convenience, and every historian inevitably uses it in accordance with his own interpretation of the recorded course of social development. But unless the term is to lose all significance, it should at least be reserved for some definite form of social order, and the modern tendency to speak of feudalism in England under Edward the Confessor may easily lead to confusion of thought. Knighthood in pre-Conquest England had few representatives beyond the garrisons of the castles built by the Confessor's French dependants, and the English antipathy to these men had deep foundations. For the differences between English society in King Edward's time and that of any part of contemporary France were fundamental, and the result of centuries of contrasted development. Within each society there still survived conceptions once general throughout the whole Germanic world. The relationship between lord and man was as common in pre-Conquest England as anywhere in France. But in England this relationship was only one element in a social order based essentially on hereditary status, and in France it had become the basis of a new type of society organized specifically for war. No process of evolution could have bridged the gap between two societies thus contrasted, and indeed, when something more than due emphasis has been laid on the signs of social change in pre-Conquest England—the leases granted by great ecclesiastics to thegns or *cnihts*, the increasing dependence of free men on lords, even the appearance of a new military element in Cnut's housecarles—the essential difference between English and Norman society remains as wide as ever. It is turning a useful term into a mere abstraction to apply the adjective "feudal" to a society which had never adopted the private fortress nor developed the art of fighting on horseback, which had no real conception of the specialization of service, and allowed innumerable landowners of position to go with their land to whatever lords they would.

6 FROM *C. Warren Hollister*
Anglo-Saxon Military Institutions

The passage below presents an interpretation of the Anglo-Saxon Worcester evidence that differs from that of Sir Frank Stenton.

Ever since the late nineteenth century there has been an exceptional amount of interest in the land leases or land loans granted by the bishops of Worcester. This has been especially true of the series of about. seventy leases granted by Bishop Oswald in the triple hundred of Oswaldslaw between 962 and 992. Almost all these leases were for three lives, that is, for the life of the grantee, that of his heir, and that of his heir's heir. V. H. Galbraith believes that some of the leases of late-Saxon times were hereditary, although this is a matter that cannot be proven conclusively. There is also some uncertainty as to the terms according to which the leases were held. What did the grantee owe the grantor in return for the lease? Maitland discusses this matter at some length. He finds that the conditions of the lease, as set forth in the individual charters, are discouragingly vague. The fealty and service of the grantee are usually mentioned, but in such a way as to imply that the lease was granted in return for *past* service. As Maitland expresses it, "Any thing that could be

SOURCE. C. Warren Hollister, *Anglo-Saxon Military Institutions*, Oxford: The Clarendon Press, 1962, pp. 98–102. Reprinted by permission of The Clarendon Press, Oxford.

called a stipulation for future service is very rare." Nevertheless, he contends that these leases were an anticipation of post-Conquest feudalism. "Dependent tenure is here," he writes, "and, we may say, feudal tenure, and even tenure by knight's service. . . ."

It should be remembered that these words were written only a short time after the publication of Round's famous essay on the introduction of knight service into England. They are intended as a rebuttal to Round's contention that knight service and the feudal military system were introduced into England by William the Conqueror and were in no way anticipated during late-Saxon times. Maitland argues that the Worcester leases were indeed such an anticipation. He bases his contention on a memorandum written by Oswald to King Edgar which Maitland regards as "for our purposes the most important of all the documents that have come down to us from the age before the Conquest." This letter sets forth in some detail the conditions on which Oswald granted his leases. The grantees are to fulfil the whole law of riding (*equitandi lex*); they are to pay church dues; they are to swear, so long as they hold their land, to be humbly subject to the commands of the bishop; they are to lend him their horses, ride for him themselves, build bridges, burn lime, erect a hedge for the bishop's hunt, lend him their hunting spears, and, in general, meet many other needs of the bishops whether for the fulfilment of the service due to him or of that due to the king. Maitland feels that these obligations are distinctly feudal in character: the grantee is the bishop's man—his *fidelis;* he owes definite services in return for his land.

"But above all, he is a horseman, a riding man and must fulfil 'the law of riding.' For a moment we are tempted to say 'the law of chivalry.' This indeed would be an anachronism; but still he is bound to ride at the bishop's command. Will he ride only on peaceful errands? We doubt it. He is bound to do all the service that is due to the king, all the forinsec service we may say. A certain quantity of military service is due from the bishop's lands; his thegns must do it. As already said, the obligation of serving in warfare is not yet so precisely connected with the tenure of certain parcels of land as it will be in the days of Henry II, but already the notion prevails that the land owes soldiers to the king, and probably the bishop has so arranged matters that his territory will be fully 'acquitted' if his *equites*, his *milites* take the field."

Maitland concludes, "It may well be that the thegns and knights of other churches held on terms very similar to those that the bishop of Worcester imposed," and that therefore, presumably, English feudalism, at least in its essentials, antedated the Conquest.

Maitland's views have been challenged vigorously by subsequent historians. Round later observed in connexion with Maitland's writings, "It is probably little realised how much conjecture and hypothesis have found their way into the work of this brilliant scholar," and Stenton devoted a section of his *First Century of English Feudalism* to a refutation of Maitland's views on pre-Conquest feudalism. . . .

It seems to me that Stenton's criticism is just, up to a point. At least from the standpoint of military organization Bishop Oswald's memorandum tells us very little. It tells us merely that the bishop's grantees owned horses and knew how to ride them. One can hardly dispute with Maitland that mounted men would be helpful on a military campaign, but the "law of riding" does not relate explicitly to military service. What, then, is the military service expected of these grantees? It is not to be found in Oswald's letter, but rather in the individual grants themselves, for almost all of these grants specifically reserve the *trimoda necessitas*.[1] Bridge-building is mentioned in the memorandum, but we know from the charters that these grantees owed fortress work and fyrd service as well. And, as we have seen, the fyrd duty of the *trimoda necessitas* consisted of service in the select fyrd.[2] The five-hide unit is common throughout the see of Wor-

---

[1] The three "necessary" obligations to the king that recur in Anglo-Saxon documents: (1) bridge building, (2) fortress work, and (3) military service —"fyrd" duty.

[2] The "select fyrd" is defined as that portion of the Anglo-Saxon army which is recruited territorially by the general obligation that every five hides of land owed one warrior to the king's fyrd when is was summoned. In some portions of England, the territorial recruitment units were standardized at figures other than five hides, but the principle remained the same.

cester, and here, as elsewhere, it constituted the basic recruitment unit. The military obligation of the Worcester lessees was simply the select-fyrd obligation which was normally due from the land: each five-hide unit produced a warrior-representative when the select fyrd was summoned. When they granted their leases, the bishops of Worcester were anxious that the alienated lands should continue to produce their required warriors. It was the bishop, as we have seen, who was responsible for raising the select-fyrd quota due from all his estates. St. Oswald's memorandum serves as convincing negative evidence that the see of Worcester placed no unusual military burden on its men. It simply expected them to do what was customary. It expected every five hides under its jurisdiction to produce a warrior.

One further point needs clarification. It has been suggested by some writers that the post-Conquest feudal military obligation was somehow more exact—mor specific—than that of the late-Saxon fyrd. This is, perhaps, the implication of Stenton's statement that, "At every critical point in the memorandum, its language shades off into vague assertions of general obligation." But it should be clear from what I have previously said that this was decidedly not the case. The obligation of military service in the select fyrd was at least as specific as the feudal military obligation. The fact that the individual Worcester leases do not specify in so many words the amount of military service owed by the grantee should not mislead us. The amount was known. It was determined by custom and could be easily calculated from the number of hides in the tenement. By virtue of the five-hide recruitment system, the fyrd obligation was just as specific as the later feudal obligation, and was at the same time considerably more systematic. The fact that every feudal charter stipulates the number of *milites*[3] owed to the lord does not indicate that the feudal obligation was more exact, but rather that it was less uniform than that of the select fyrd. The latter was national in scope and was based on a standard relationship between land and service. The former was based on individual fees which varied among themselves in both hidage and military obligation and which were created by discrete private contracts. These feudal

[3] Knights.

contracts were of the nature of bargains, for in the absence of any accepted ratio of hides to service the feudal lord would be likely to demand whatever he could get. Consequently, the amount of service is always specified in a feudal contract but almost never in an Anglo-Saxon land charter. The military structure of late-Saxon England differs from that of Norman England, but not in the way that many historians have thought.

As to the aptness of the term *feudal* to describe the pre-Conquest military system, I would prefer not to commit myself. Feudalism can be and has been defined in a bewildering variety of ways. Let us say merely that an important Anglo-Saxon lord owed the service of an exact number of warriors as a result of his tenement. But the same land would owe the same service whether held by one lord, several lords, or no lord at all. The military obligation of the Anglo-Saxon nobleman was therefore merely one aspect of a larger structure—a national structure—which in other aspects was far less reminiscent of the feudal military arrangements of the Continent. As a whole, the Old-English system was decidedly unlike that of Norman feudalism. Was it feudal at all? That question I will leave to others who may be more certain than I as to how feudalism ought to be defined.

PART FOUR

The Modern Controversy Over
The Round Hypothesis

1 FROM *Marjory Hollings, The Introduction to Volume IV of The Red Book of Worcester*

It was on the basis of still additional historical evidence from the bishopric of Worcester that the first major scholarly counterattack against Round's hypothesis was mounted. Marjory Hollings first presented her argument in a scholarly article, "The Survival of the Five-Hide Unit in the Western Midlands," English Historical Review, LXIII (1948). The remarks below are taken from a subsequent work, her introduction to the fourth and last volume of her edition of The Red Book of Worcester *(1950). On the basis of this evidence she argued that the territorial units of five hides, which constituted the basis of pre-Conquest English military recruitment, are found in Worcester to constitute the basis of knights' fees long after the Conquest. Accordingly, she sees an important degree of continuity in military tenures across the line of 1066. Her attempt to show a similar continuity in the bishop of Worcester's military quota to the king is highly technical and altogether less successful.*

It has hitherto been generally agreed that . . . the Norman conqueror introduced a system of military service which at every point ignored Old English precedent, since the amount of service which King William demanded from his tenants in chief bore no definite relation to the extent or value of their lands. Very few details, however, have been so far made available about the actual make-up of the new Norman fees, and therefore the twelfth-century notes on this subject, contained in the Miscellanea,[1] are of exceptional interest. They include the earliest extant lists of the bishop's knights; a series of notes apparently intended to show

[1] A section of *The Red Book of Worcester.*

SOURCE. Marjory Hollings, ed., *The Red Book of Worcester*, London: Worcestershire Historical Society, 1934–1950, Vol. IV, pp. xx–xxiii, xxv–xxvii, xxxv, and xxxvii. Reprinted by permission of the Worcestershire Historical Society.

how his quota of fees was constituted in 1166; a memorandum, made evidently for St. Wulfstan after the Norman Conquest, concerning the ungeldable hides in his demesne; and the return of the knights' fees held of the bishop in 1208. . . .

The earliest lists of the bishop's knights . . . are . . . likely to have been drawn up for Bishop John of Pageham (1151-8) in support of the claim, maintained also by his successors, that he had been assessed at more than his due service: which was properly fifty, not sixty, knights. . . . Most of the information about the make-up of the fees is contained in . . . notes, evidently compiled for Bishop Roger of Gloucester,[2] together with a memorandum interpolated in the return of 1208 between the fees held under William de Beauchamp and those held directly of the bishop. ·

According to this memorandum: "Four yardlands make one hide,[3] and five hides provide one knight." The point, as Round maintained, "is of importance, because if we found that the recognised area of a knight's fee was five hides, it would give us a link between the under-tenant (*miles*) and the Anglo-Saxon thegn," and indicate that English feudalism was not the conscious creation of alien conquerors, but a development of Saxon fyrd service and the product of centuries of growth.

The assertion in the memorandum is everywhere borne out by Roger of Gloucester's notes, which record: In Worcestershire: "Tredyntone, Ralf Travers four hides, William Haket at Alvechurch one hide, they provide a knight." In Gloucestershire: "Sampson, half a knight, and with him Philip of Colesbourne two hides and Walter of Bibury half a hide; they provide a knight." Even in Warwickshire, where the bishop had less land and the fee had to be made up outside the county, five hides are required to form the knight's fee: "Frederic of Bishopsdon one knight . . . and of this tenure in Stratford three hides, in Fladbury two hides."

The same principle is noticeable in respect of the great fiefs which supplied many knights to the bishop's quota: "The sum of all the hides which William . (de Beauchamp) holds of the bishop in the said three counties is a hundred and nine and a half

---

[2] Roger of Gloucester was bishop of Worcester from 1164 to 1179.
[3] The hide was traditionally divisible into four "yardlands" or "virgates."

. . . He says he holds all these of the Bishop as the fee of fifteen knights, when there is the fee of twenty-two knights at least, except half a hide." "The sum of the whole (Bohun fee) is thirty-seven geldable hides, which ought to provide the fee of seven knights and a half, if half a hide be added."

The survival of five hides as the unit of military service is perhaps even more clearly shown by the small holdings. There is here a good deal of repetition, for the list of these fees has apparently been written three or four times, with various suggested combinations to provide a knight; and it is even possible that it represents an amalgamation of notes made for earlier bishops than Roger. The principle on which the fee is to be constructed, however, remains the same, and references to the tenure of five hides as providing for a knight are also to be found in the extents, even in the latest of the surveys made for Godfrey Giffard, that of 1299. Clearly there must have been some reason less cataclysmic than the complete supersession of the Anglo-Saxon system to account for the variation in the knight's fee which led to the belief that the amount of service demanded by King William bore no definite relation to the extent or value of his tenant's lands. This reason is probably to be found partly in the local variations of pre-Conquest custom; partly in the retention of an archaic system of changing land values and an individual tampering with the hidage; and partly in an incomplete establishment of the Norman usage of military service, which allowed the earlier English system in some respects to survive.

The evidence of the Red Book of the bishopric makes necessary a fresh examination of the problem which, it is hoped, will throw new light on the incidence of military service, both before and after the Conquest. A convenient starting point is to be found in a discussion of the hidage of the bishop's lands and the quota of knights imposed on them. The memorandum of St. Wulfstan[4] has a direct bearing on the existence of ungeldable hides and the immunity of the demesne; and it was probably for this reason that it was copied into his successor's book of fees, although the arithmetic is not always sound. The comparatively simple addition

[4] Bishop of Worcester, 1062–1095.

of the ungeldable hides is, however, correct. These hides, twenty-four and a quarter in number, lay in those districts which at the time of the survey for Domesday Book contained a large proportion of marsh, downland, or wood, and are later shown to have been still in process of intake during the last half of the thirteenth century. They did not geld, as the memorandum tells us, because they had not been included in the ancient hidage; and this appears also to have prevented them from supporting *milites*, at least as long as the pre-Conquest system of military service continued in use. Evidently they were regarded as exempt in the time of Roger of Gloucester, when ten ungeldable hides in Fladbury were recorded in connexion with Hugh de Lacy's claim to hold twenty hides there for two knights' fees.

The ungeldable hides were not, however, the only reduction to be made from the bishop's total of 524 before his due service could be determined. The demesne land of a manor was not liable to support a warrior other than its lord, and early enfeoffments often imply that it is from the dependent tenements, *terra villanorum*, that knights' fees are to be formed, and that land *de victu proprio*[5] ought to be excluded from grants for military service, although temporary grants of it might sometimes be made. Unfortunately we are not given quite the necessary data for an exact estimate of the immune demesne. The meaning of the statement that the bishop has in demesne one hundred and sixteen hides and one yardland, besides the hides which freemen hold, is not quite clear; but the reference to the hides already held by freemen makes it seem on the whole probable that these hides still in demesne were the remainder left after the demesne *de victu* had been subtracted. Of this number twenty-four hides and one yardland were, as we have seen, ungeldable, so that the number actually available for enfeoffment would have been ninety-two hides. If to these we add the number held in 1086 by those knights whose

---

[5] The distinction between *terra villanorum* (villain's land) and land *de victu proprio* (for the maintenance of the bishop himself) is simply the distinction between land by peasants and manorial demesne land exploited directly by the lord (in this case the bishop of Worcester). The highly technical analysis that follows has failed to convince most scholars that a relationship existed between the total hides of the bishopric of Worcester's estates and the bishop's feudal military quota.

predecessors had thegnlands of the bishop, the total is 258 hides; rather more than the fifty fees which the bishops of Worcester declared were their quota. If, however, we add the ungeldable land and the land held in 1086 by the radmen who (although they held of the old enfeoffment) were not considered military tenants in the time of Henry II, the number is increased by about fifty hides, another ten fees; from which it would appear that the bishop's due service was to supply the sixty knights at which he had been assessed. It is therefore not surprising that the claim put forward by Bishop John of Pageham in 1156 to provide only fifty knights was not at first admitted, and that Roger of Gloucester was still pursuing it ten years later. Its ultimate success was perhaps due as much to the bishop's influence with the crown as to the merits of his case; but the see had lost a good deal of land since the ancient assessment, and the bishop seems to have had reason to believe that the disputed number of knights should have been supplied by the great tenants who had acquired the property. . . .

However the quota may have been decided, it was not strictly in accordance with the hidage, but was regarded as having been settled once for all before the death of St. Wulfstan in 1095. An earlier date is probable, since the fact that the King himself is entered in Domesday Book as the bishop's tenant of the two fees in Bushley, Barely, Queenhill and Pull, implies that the bishop's quota must have been fixed by 1086. Evidence from other ecclesiastical lands supports this earlier date for the final decision: the bishop of Hereford had settled his quota, or most of it, on his land by 1085, and the full *servicium debitum* of Evesham Abbey is recorded, in working order, as early as 1072.

It does not, however, necessarily follow from this conclusion that the military obligations of the great churchmen were in the first instance arbitrarily fixed by the will of the Conqueror. There had been tampering with the hidage of ecclesiastical lands for more than a century before the Norman Conquest, and King William, subjected on all sides to the pressure of affairs, may well have felt it advisable to take such service as had been acknowledged in the time of King Edward. It is to be noted that where the dispute about an "unacknowledged fee" can be traced to its origin, it is usually found to relate, not to the terms on which the Domesday tenant received the land, but to those on which it had been held by his English *antecessor*; and there is more than one record of the undertaking by a Norman of his predecessor's obligations. The majority of the Worcester fees constituted "of old"[6] had been thegnlands held of the church, many of them from the time of Bishop Oswald (961-92): an indication that local custom may have helped to determine the number of knights which the King demanded.

It is true that there appears to have been no uniformity in the assessment of the tenants in chief for knight service, but it is also true that there was no uniformity of custom in the England of the eleventh century; and although the most violent discrepancies are not explained by any proportionate differences in either the value or the extent of the lands, they are in many instances explained by special privileges. An original idea of uniformity may perhaps be postulated from the fact that quotas of forty or more knights were generally imposed on most baronies of over £200 annual value, and quotas of between twenty and forty on baronies with an annual income of £100 to £200; but the question of due service was everywhere complicated by altered land values and reductions in the hidage made by favour or encroachment. . . .

It is clear, however, that such reductions in the hidage were by no means a Norman innovation, for they can be traced back before the Conquest. Bishop Ealdred (1044-62) had granted to his thegn Wulfgeat for three lives a hide and a half at Ditchford in Blockley, "and at the King's summons the holder shall redeem it at the rate of one hide"; and to Æthelstan the Fat he had made a similar grant of two hides at Hill in Fladbury, "along with what he had before, and with the land without houses; and he shall answer for them at the rate of two hides." . . .

There is perhaps hardly enough evidence to enable us to judge of the extent to which social developments in our district were disturbed by the Conquest. By 1066 many of Oswald's grants

---

[6] "Of old" in this case means prior to the death of Bishop Wulfstan of Worcester in 1095.

must have been nearing their end, and it was in order to safeguard his overlordship that St. Wulfstan caused copies of them to be inserted in the great Bible which Offa had given to the cathedral church. Certain passages in Heming's cartulary[7] and in Domesday Book suggest that the bishop's tenants in possession were more or less undisturbed, and that Norman encroachments on the land of the church were usually, though not always, made when a grant had run out. It is recorded in Domesday Book that one Norman at least based his claim on the ground that the previous tenant had been the last in the grant; but it is not improbable that others brought pressure to bear on some of the landed thegns to choose a foreign heir, for we find Ralf de Mortimer and Urse d'Abitot[8] each named as the third life in possession of a thegnland in 1086. This implies that they held the land on the same terms as their predecessors, and there is definite evidence that they were not the only Normans willing to enter into such agreements. . . .

The continuity of the old English system is shown not only by the survival of the five-hide unit, but in the actual tenure of former thegnlands by foreigners as well as Englishmen after the Conquest. Ealdred's grants for lives have much in common with early enfeoffments, and the enfeoffment made by Robert, Bishop of Hereford, in 1085 is in effect the renewal of a grant for life. The riding service was commuted early, but the freeholders who succeeded to the radmen's tenements succeeded also to some of the duties of the lesser thegns, as their lords did to those of the greater; and the quasi-beneficiary tenure lingered on ecclesiastical estates for many years. The longer term of service demanded by English custom was a definite advantage to the Crown; and it is evident that in some districts of England at least King William adopted the local system of military tenure much as he found it.

Finally, it is clear that in the most important point of difference between the Anglo-Saxon system and the Norman, the Conqueror's settlement, so far from ignoring old English precedent, was actually based upon it.

---

[7] An important Worcester record.
[8] Two great Norman barons of the Conqueror's era.

2 FROM   *Eric John*
Land Tenure in Early England

In this provocative work, published in 1960, the cautious attack of Marjory Hollings against the "feudal revolution" hypothesis was escalated into a full-scale onslaught.

English historians since the days of Round have always placed much weight on the origin of the quotas of knights which Anglo-Norman tenants in chief contributed to make up the host, and they have treated it as the determining factor for or against continuity. It is now almost unquestioned that these quotas were imposed on the Anglo-Norman tenants in chief by William the Conqueror, as an essential and early part of the Conquest settlement. Believing this, it is very difficult for scholars to accept the possibility that the Anglo-Saxon *fyrd* could really have been raised in a similar way to the host.[1] Even Maitland, who saw so much evidence of feudal arrangements in pre-Conquest society, was not prepared to admit that the resemblance could be more than that of an embryonic feudalism to the fully matured system of Henry II's day. This was largely because he thought the feudal host was invented by the Conqueror. It is not the least interesting consequence of the Worcester evidence that this widely held opinion can be seriously questioned. The opinion was, of course, the subject of Round's most famous paper, "The Introduction of Knight Service into England," where it was defended with a set of arguments as dazzling as they were ingenious. There can be

[1] I.e., the post-Conquest Anglo-Norman feudal host.

SOURCE. Eric John, *Land Tenure in Early England*, Leicester: Leicester University Press, 1960, pp. 149–159. Copyright 1960 by Eric John. Reprinted by permission of Leicester University Press, Humanities Press, and the author.

no doubt that the paper represents a major advance in the subject of the origin of the quotas. It is by any standards a magnificent piece of work; but one may question whether it proves as much as it has been held to prove. Indeed, Round's argument proves nothing, because it is circular. This is not to say that it is false, but it is the kind of argument that illuminates but does not prove anything, and its cogency depends entirely on its apparently unique ability to throw light on the origin of the quotas. The argument is of a type used very rarely by medieval historians, an inference from a set of statistics to a matter of fact. Round had the brilliant idea of listing the quotas of traditional knight service as returned by the English tenants in chief to the inquest of 1166. When the quotas were listed, it became apparent that most of them are round numbers divisible by five; some of them are also divisible by ten. Round inferred from this that the uniformity of the quotas required a basic principle to explain it, and could only have been achieved if the quotas had been imposed by a strong central authority, that is, some king prior to Henry II's reign. So far there is nothing to disagree with. Round further argued for a *terminus ante quem* on grounds which are fairly strong. He cited, and printed, a writ of the Conqueror to Abbott Æthelwig of Evesham, which summoned Æthelwig and his quota of five knights. This is the quota admitted by the Evesham monks in 1166. The writ cannot be later than 1077, the year of Æthelwig's death, and is most probably to be dated no later than 1072. Since the quota is the same in 1072 as in 1166; and since it is an absolutely characteristic quota, there is reason to suppose that the principle of uniformity had been devised and applied by 1072. The crux of the argument, however, turns on the *terminus a quo*, and it is here that Round's argument runs into difficulties he did not foresee, though, as will presently appear, Freeman saw some of them at the time.

Round set out to find an explanation of the uniformity behind the quotas, and he found some very feeble literary evidence suggesting that the ducal host in Normandy was composed of *constabulariae* or squadrons of ten men. This he put forward as the explanation of the English quotas; they had been so imposed as to provide an English version of the ducal host, a nexus of *constabulariae*. The only king who could have legislated for *con-*

stabulariae before 1072 was William the Conqueror, and it also looked as though he must have done this very early in his reign, which is indeed entirely probable if he did it at all. But the argument loses all its force if it can be shown on the one hand that the *constabularia* does not explain the figures, and, on the other, that the late Old English *fyrd* was raised in quotas of ten thegns. The *constabularia* has a very limited power of explanation. All we know about it is that the host may have fought as a set of squadrons of ten knights, but this does not necessarily mean that the host was raised in quotas of ten. To argue from military convenience to the original assessment requires the assistance of a hypothesis, namely that the quotas must have matched the *constabulariae* because in feudal conditions the men must have fought under the banner of their lord, and therefore a feudal host could only achieve *constabulariae* of ten men if the quotas were likewise composed. If this is so, then how can the *constabularia* explain the quotas of five men in the English list? Under whose banner did these half-*constabulariae* serve? Some of them cannot have served under their own lord, and if this was tolerable what becomes of the link between *constabularia* and quota? Further, once quotas allow for fractions of *constabulariae*, why stop at half? It is no more difficult to make up an odd *constabularia* by combining quotas of six and four than it is by adding two quotas of five. In any case, it is not likely that all the men due to serve could have turned up sound in wind and limb at the exact time they were required.

There are, then, difficulties in the way of putting such weight on the *constabularia*. But there is one very simple and to my mind decisive objection to Round's argument, and that is the character of the Norman quotas. These were returned in 1172, and like the English quotas were recorded in the *Red Book of the Exchequer*. Haskins lists the episcopal quotas in his *Norman Institutions*, and he remarks: "The *servitia debita* of this list are smaller than those of the English bishops and abbots, and perhaps for this reason, the group of five knights is not quite so much in evidence." This is an understatement: the group of five knights is not in evidence at all. The quotas of the Norman ecclesiastical tenants run, in the order Haskins prints them: 10, 5, 20, 6, 20, 10, 3, 6¾, 7, 1, 2 or 3, 4, 6, 2, 1, 3. The lay quotas show no greater uniformity; some quotas are divisible by five or ten, but many are not. The Norman quotas, both ecclesiastical and lay, are in general much smaller than the English. It is difficult to believe that the principle behind the English quotas can also explain the Norman figures, which do not seem to be reckoned on any principle at all.

Before Round wrote, Freeman had produced an objection to the claim of the Conqueror to have introduced these quotas, which indeed Round knew, since he cited it in a *catena* of quotations selected from Stubbs and Gneist, as well as Freeman, for anathema. Freeman wrote: "There is no ground for thinking that William directly or systematically introduced any new kind of tenure into the holding of English lands. There is nothing to suggest any such belief, either in the chronicles of his reign, in the Survey, which is his greatest monument, in the genuine or even in the spurious remains of his legislation." This silence in an age full of excellent chroniclers, and loud with the complaints of the clergy, takes some explaining. The abbey of St. Augustine's, for instance, answered for fifteen knights; it also had a set of chroniclers with the keenest interest in the *minutiae* of the business of their abbey. Two columns of Twysden are devoted to the loss of ordinary jurisdiction suffered by the abbey in the time of Lanfranc, which amounted to no more than that the priests who served the abbey's churches had to attend the archbishop's synod. Even more parchment was spent on an early twelfth-century lawsuit which lost the monks little more than a pound a year, yet of the imposition of the quota of knights there is no word. Another curious silence is that of Archbishop Anselm in his first quarrel with Rufus. . . .

The piece of chronicle evidence that does unequivocally support Round's thesis is a passage from Matthew Paris, which is usually cited as witness "to the tradition." Since Matthew declares that before William's reign English bishoprics and abbeys had been free of all secular services, he plainly does not know what he is talking about; when he speaks of setting down the quotas in rolls, he may be quoting a confused memory of the Domesday survey, or even the inquest of 1166. Against the late and ill-informed statement of Matthew Paris, the silence of Orderic Vitalis and Eadmer is an argument of weight.

But the greatest lacuna in Round's thesis was his failure to ascertain, even roughly, how the Anglo-Saxon *fyrd* was raised. He seems to have supposed that the hidage of the estate was totted up and then divided by five, the result being led out to the *fyrd*. If this were so, then plainly the Anglo-Saxon system could rarely if ever have provided quotas divisible by five and ten. But the Oswaldslow and Taunton evidence, supplemented by some evidence from Domesday pointed out by Round himself, puts the raising of the *fyrd* in a very different light. Round supposed that the principle used was the five-hide unit alone, but this is not so: the five-hide unit must be taken along with what seems to have been the most important unit from the king's standpoint, the hundred.

The hundred is, of course, older than Edgar's day. Its court, it is true, cannot be taken back beyond Edward the Elder or Alfred, and the bringing of the tithing groups into the hundred is no older than the ordinance of the Hundred; but continental analogy, and the names of some of the hundreds, which go back to pre-christian times, suggest that the tenth-century hundred had a long ancestry. Professor Stenton, moreover, has pointed out that there are traces of the unit of a hundred hides behind the primitive *regiones* of the Mercian supremacy and before. "If a *regio* were to be divided, it would tend to fall into districts each of which would answer for a round one hundred hides when the king took his *feorm* or called out his *fyrd*." Chadwick also noted that in the Tribal Hidage, an early tribute list from the time of the Mercian hegemony,[2] "the number of hides allotted to the various units are in all cases multiples of 100." We have no evidence which enables us to say much about the early hundred beyond that it existed before the Viking wars, but with the establishment of the burghal system, probably by Alfred,[3] and the appearance of the document drawn up in connexion with it, the Burghal Hidage, which probobly dates from the reign of Edward the Elder,[4] we are on firmer ground. Many of the assessments attached to the *burhs*[5] in the list are composed of round numbers of

[2] The eighth century.
[3] Alfred reigned 871–899.
[4] 899–925. Edward the Elder was Alfred's son.
[5] Fortified centers.

hundreds of hides, and there is no reason to doubt that in Edwardian times a *burh* was the centre of a grouping of hundreds. In two cases, Worcester with its 1,200 hides, Oxford with its 2,400 hides; Worcestershire with its twelve hundreds, Oxfordshire with its twenty-four hundreds, there is a significant parallel between the figures of the Burghal Hidage, and the composition of the shires in Domesday Book. The Burghal Hidage suggests, then, that the new defence system of Alfred and his son was based on a variant of the traditional *regio* or hundred. The subsequent history of the hundred is probably connected in some way with that of the *burh*, and both have their place in the making of Edgar's shipfuls.[6] At any rate, in Edgar's day there appears a court called *burhgemot*, and a law of Cnut,[7] II Cnut, 22.1, reveals that the area of jurisdiction of a *burh* may have been three hundreds. C. S. Taylor's important paper, "The Origin of the Mercian Shires," shows that the Mercian shires were in fact shaped from a combination of the burghal and shipful systems. We have already seen from the Oswaldslow evidence that the hundred was a unit of military organization.[8] The Oswaldslow evidence again suggests that so far as the king was concerned, a hundred was a parcel of twenty thegns liable for the *fyrd*. By Edgar's reign it had become rather a complicated parcel, transformed by the necessities of the times into a series of trinities, or shipfuls. CS 1135[9] also shows that not only were these shipfuls raised by traditional representatives of the king, the ealdorman, and the hundred exactors, but that at least as early as Edgar all power over them under the king was sometimes delegated to bishops. CS 1135 also shows that some kind of hundredal au-

---

[6] The "shipfuls" are units of 300 hides owing (at the rate of one man from five hides) a sixty-man ship's crew to the king's navy. Evidence suggests that the shipful system may have flourished under King Edgar (959–975).

[7] Reigned 1016–1035.

[8] Oswaldslow was an extensive territory of the bishop of Worcester, rated at 300 hides for military and other purposes. Mr. John regards it as a characteristic "shipful" and it is commonly termed a "triple hundred."

[9] Document number 1135 in a printed collection of Anglo-Saxon records known as *Cartularium Saxonicum*. The document in question, purporting to have been granted to the bishopric of Worcester by King Edgar in 964, describes the privileges of the bishop's triple hundred of Oswaldslow.

thority might be exercised by a private lord before Bishop Oswald's time, but that it was of a lesser kind. Putting all this together, I think we can see a dim outline of the way in which the system of delegation worked. Hundreds might be granted away but this may not in itself have conveyed military powers. These are more likely, but not certainly, to have been reserved until a full shipful was granted. What is plain is that the king raised his *fyrd* in quotas which, being based on the hundred, must have been divisible by five or ten. Further, these quotas are likely to have been of the order of twenty and sixty men; any one who compares the list of English knight service in 1166 with the Norman list of 1172 cannot but be struck by the much greater size of the English quotas, and the number of quotas which were multiples of twenty. . . .

. . . It is now fairly clear that the Anglo-Saxon system [like the Norman system] was also imposed from the top in units divisible by ten, and that the hidage and the five-hide unit are subservient to the more important hundredal unit. This was neatly shown by Round himself in a comment on a passage from the Domesday account of Bedford. According to *DB*, Bedford "T.R.E. pro dimidio hundred se defendebat:"[10] that is "in expeditione et in navibus."[11] Round himself pointed out this probably meant that Bedford produced ten men for the *fyrd*. Further, "Terra de hac villa nunquam fuit hidata."[12] Thus we have clear proof that the hundredal assessment, the quota, came first and the hidage second, or perhaps not at all. And the Worcester evidence strongly suggests that the splitting of the hundred into its component thegnlands, the detailed hidation of the area, lay within the power of the head of the new hundred or shipful. . . .

. . . The arguments adduced by Round to prove that William the Conqueror invented the system of English knight service will not hold. It seems, further, that the principle on which the quotas in the inquest of 1166 were originally calculated must have been

---

[10] "At the time of Edward the Confessor's death, Bedford served for half a hundred."

[11] "In military and naval expeditions."

[12] "The land of this vill was never assessed in hides."

related to the system of hundreds and shipfuls.

At this point I had better confess that I cannot see how this was done. There are signs which may indicate continuity of quotas, but not many, and they are trecherous signs. The obvious place to look for signs of continuity is in the ecclesiastical quotas. The church of Worcester answered for sixty knights' traditional service in 1166, and so did the churches of Winchester and Canterbury. We know that Worcester possessed a shipful, which it got through the intercession of Dunstan of Canterbury and Æthelwold of Winchester.[13] Since shipfuls were desirable; since comparatively unfavoured sees such as Sherborne had them, it is difficult to believe that Dunstan and Æthelwold did not have them too, especially when an archbishop of Canterbury about 990 leaves his king as heriot the equipment of sixty thegns. The quotas of 1166 for these churches must, I think, have some connexion with Edgar's shipfuls. But the connexion is not straightforward. On the basis of the *Red Book of Worcester*, Miss Hollings has shown that after the Conquest, when bishops of Worcester drew up lists of their knights' fees rated in hides in the hope of getting their quota reduced, they based their calculations on the whole of the hidage of land they possessed inside and outside Oswaldslow. This is difficult. It is possible that in a sense the church of Worcester served for the whole of its estates through Oswaldslow, and that the men of other estates from which Worcester drew some kind of income answered for the *fyrd* personally. It may be that the quotas once confined to the shipfuls were allowed to stand for the whole of the Worcester, Canterbury, and Winchester estates; if so, the quota system underwent a progressive dilution between the time of Edgar and that of the Conqueror. This seems to me very much the likeliest explanation. It neither undervalues the Conqueror's power after 1066 nor underestimates the consequences of the Conquest. It merely says that we must think of the Conqueror's innovations as residing rather in his use of existing institutions than in the creation of new ones.

In any case, by 1066 the quotas were not of great military

[13] Important English prelates and ecclesiastical reformers of the tenth century.

value; the amateur gentleman-knight was not good enough for eleventh-century warfare. Mr. Lyon has shown that we must take the indenture, thinly disguised as the money-fief, back to the Anglo-Norman period, and Mr. Prestwich, in an important paper on Anglo-Norman warfare, has shown that from 1066 onwards it was mercenaries, paid for with English money, not the feudal host, which won battles for the rulers of England.[14]

3   FROM   *H. G. Richardson and G. O. Sayles*
The Governance of Mediaeval England

Here the attack against Round reaches its intellectual and emotional crescendo. Notice that although both Eric John and Richardson and Sayles agree that feudal tenures evolved gradually in England, John is inclined to think that the evolution occurred during the century prior to 1066 whereas Richardson and Sayles place the evolution in the century between 1066 and 1166—the date of Henry II's survey of knights' fees known as the Cartæ Baronum. *(See the Evesham return from the* Cartæ Baronum *printed earlier in this volume.)*

The Normans had little statecraft and little foresight. They came as conquerors, not as reformers: if they had no mind to mend their own habits and customs, they had little mind to mend the habits and customs of the conquered.

The persistence into the early twelfth century, and occasionally

[14] Bryce Lyon, *From Fief to Indenture* (Cambridge, Mass., 1958); J. O. Prestwich, "War and Finance in the Anglo-Norman State," *Transactions of the Royal Historical Society*, fifth series, IV (1954), pp. 19–43.

SOURCE. H. G. Richardson and G. O. Sayles, *The Governance of Mediaeval England from the Conquest to Magna Carta*, Edinburgh: University Press, 1963, pp. 26–28, 33, 60–66, and 90–91. Reprinted by permission of Edinburgh University Press.

into the reign of Henry II, of English charters and English writs should indicate to us, as surely as the persistence of English institutions, that for half a century or so from 1066 the English way of life was not sensibly altered. The Normans had very little to teach, even in the art of war, and they had very much to learn. They were barbarians who were becoming conscious of their insufficiency. Under William the Conqueror nearly all the dioceses, nearly all the larger abbeys of Normandy, had at their head an Italian or a Lotharingian. If the Normans were more aware of their deficiencies in the Church than in the State, it was not because they were skilled in the arts of government. They were not great administrators: in their small barbaric province they had never been seriously confronted with the problems of administration. They made shift with the relics of earlier systems of government and some later improvisations. In a sense this is true of all mediaeval states, but the English state of the eleventh century was, by contrast with them, an ordered polity, and an ordered polity, unless it is completely disrupted by an invader, is likely, as so many historical examples testify, to persist, to survive the dislocation of foreign and civil war. And despite his barbaric devastation of much of his new kingdom, Duke William was of a mind to preserve what he regarded as his inheritance. We may add that, if the Conqueror's will had prevailed and the dukedom of Normandy had gone to his eldest son and his line and the kingdom of England to his second son and his line, the Norman Conquest would have been a transitory episode and the foreign element it had introduced would, we make bold to say, have been absorbed into English society almost without trace. The Scandinavian conquest, earlier in the eleventh century, is a telling parallel.

That the Normans had little statecraft and little foresight, that they had very little to teach and very much to learn, seems to us the obvious conclusion from their history; but so to declare is, we recognise, to fly in the face of the settled convictions of successive generations of historians to whom the Conqueror has appeared as a heroic figure of almost superhuman proportions. Nor did he lack panegyrists of his own time, not least the Peterborough monk who had resided for a while at his court and to whom he seemed exceedingly wise and of great nobility, more worshipful and commanding than any of his predecessors.[1] But these praises are outweighed by the catalogue of the king's faults, his egotism, his cruelty, his greed and his avarice, the very negation of ideal kingship. William, indeed, seems to have been astute without wisdom, resolute without foresight, powerful without ultimate purpose, a man of very limited aims and very limited vision, narrow, ignorant and superstitious. Of the pattern of his Norse ancestors, he was inferior to the greater among them and—to draw a particular comparison—he was morally and intellectually on a much lower plane than Cnut. . . .

Foreign influences, therefore, were more apparent than real in modifying the character of the English monarchy, while below the seat of power the changes at first were few or none; and when change did come, it was not the result of foreign influence but as a response to the needs of good government. Thus, the county and hundred courts continued and so, it would seem, did the courts it is convenient to call manorial, although "manor" is not a term to be found in England before 1066. If the post-Conquest earls lose the extensive powers of pre-Conquest earls, the sheriff remains the local representative of the central government. The revenues of the English kings become the revenues of the Norman kings, although they are supplemented by revenues arising out of feudal incidents. The witan continues, if with an altered complexion, as the king's council. The structure of the state remains essentially as it was, modified perhaps, but not changed in any fundamental element, to accommodate any new ideas of the relationship between lord and vassal which the Normans brought with them. . . .

Landed or not, the knight, before and after the Conquest, was a mounted soldier, more or less effectively armoured. The richer he was, the better mounted, the better armed, the better armoured. As time went on, it was the richer men to whom the title of knight was exclusively given, men, that is, who were rich in

---

[1] The reference here is to the passage from the *Anglo-Saxon Chronicle* printed in this volume. See above.

land. Indeed, it became obligatory on such men to become knights or to pay for the privilege of freedom from the onerous duties that gradually accumulated upon landed knights. But at the time of the Conquest the distinction between an English *cniht* and a Norman *chivaler* was not that the latter was richer or better mounted or armed: they were not different in much else than speech and culture. "Harold dux Anglorum et milites sui[2] figure prominently at the beginning of the Bayeux Tapestry. If these English knights—as we do not hesitate so to translate the Latin—had not been labelled, we might excusably have mistaken them for Norman *chivalers*. The designer of the tapestry, who is credibly believed to have lived within living memory of the events it depicts, failed to see the sharp distinction that has become apparent to modern historians. If he were blind, we prefer to share his blindness. And then, as it seems to us, other contemporary witnesses failed equally to distinguish, except in the matter of race and speech, between English and French, and even here they stumbled occasionally. *Milites* are to be found widely scattered over Domesday Book. There we find a good many English *milites*, just as we find French thegns in the Exon Domesday,[3] though men of the same class are apt to be called thegns without qualification if they are English and *milites* if they are French. Though all are freemen, these French knights are of all social grades, from substantial landowners, the equivalent of the English five-hide thegns, to men who had to be content with a small holding that put them on a level with the English peasant. French knights were no class apart: they fitted into the vacant places, high and low, among the defeated and dispossessed English people. And it is desirable at this point to emphasise that,

---

[2] "Harold duke (or earl) of the English and his soldiers (or knights)." The word *miles* (plural: *milites*) is normally translated in records of the late eleventh century and thereafter as "knight," meaning a well-equipped warrior with a mount, trained in mounted combat. The original classical definition of the word is merely "soldier." The exact meaning of the term in immediate post-Conquest records such as Domesday Book—and the Bayeux Tapestry—is a matter of dispute. Most historians believe that the pre-Conquest English warriors were ignorant of mounted combat tactics and invariably fought on foot. It is this view that Richardson and Sayles are endeavoring to refute.

[3] A local survey related to and contemporary with Domesday Book.

so far as the evidence goes, the Norman Conquest introduced no new conceptions of warfare, no new ranks of society. It is because of their implications that it is necessary to deny such statements, made by historians of repute, as that "Harold's army was confined by its nature to a type of warfare which was already obsolete in the greater part of Western Europe" or that "the battle of Hastings was in essence the defeat of infantry by a composite force, where the cavalry manoeuvred in support of the foot-soldiers." To argue thus is to argue against the evidence. There was no revolution in the art of war and no consequent social revolution. Evidently the Conquest brought with it an almost complete displacement in the higher ranks of society: in the course of the Conqueror's reign the Old English nobility practically disappeared and were replaced by foreigners. But the process was literally a replacement: estates were not thrown into hotch-potch and then redistributed. In landholding as in government, there was continuity. What was new was a foreign system of tenure which was gradually imposed upon the old native system. It is this gradual development, not any catastrophic change, that would justify us in speaking of English feudalism. . . .

If we are to attempt a rational account of the settlement that followed the Norman Conquest, we must begin by dissipating a myth, the myth that almost immediately after his coronation King William introduced "feudalism" into England and that he did this by allotting quotas of knight service to the estates of his tenants-in-chief. So rapid was his work, we are assured, that it was accomplished before the end of 1070. The details of this remarkable feat are unfortunately wrapped in almost complete obscurity, and the belief that it was performed at all rests, not upon any contemporary authority, but solely upon an obviously erroneous assertion, more than a century later, by Roger of Wendover and the assumptions of J. H. Round. Since Round's whole thesis, which has won general acceptance, turns upon his interpretation of Wendover's words, we may give a little space to an examination of this piece of evidence.

The passage in Wendover's annal for 1070 upon which Round seized states that the Conqueror gave orders that all bishoprics and abbeys which held baronies and had hitherto been exempt from secular burdens should render knight service and that the quota, fixed arbitrarily, should be enrolled. Taken out of its setting this passage might seem worthy of serious consideration, if it could be shown to be drawn substantially from an early source. But Wendover's annal, as a whole, is nonsensical, and any statement in any part of it needs ample corroboration before it is to be believed. Among other improbabilities he states that in this year Archbishop Stigand and (the yet unborn) Alexander, bishop of Lincoln, fled to Scotland: and this is no unfair measure of Wendover's historicity. Round, it may be explained, knew Wendover's annal only through Matthew Paris's *Historia Anglorum* and, although the editor of this chronicle had given the clearest indication that Paris was merely reproducing Wendover with some embellishments, Round surmised that the passage upon which he relied "perhaps represented the St. Alban's tradition"— whatever that might mean—and it is with this feeble evidence, if evidence it can be called, that he claimed to have verified his "simple and obvious inference" that "just as Henry II granted out the provinces of Ireland to be held as fiefs by the familiar service of a round number of knights, so"—in the year 1070— "Duke William granted out the fiefs he formed in England."

Neither Round nor, indeed, very recent writers have thought it necessary to go behind Paris to Wendover or to enquire what truth may lie behind Wendover's extravagances: for all of them, whether supporters or critics of Round, Paris is the ultimate authority. And it may perhaps be thought pedantic on our part to object to reliance upon what is, at best, secondary authority when the primary authority is available; after all, Round was but following the example of Stubbs. But Round should at least have known, and his supporters should know, that the lands of bishops and abbots were not exempt from secular burdens before the Conquest, though some favoured abbeys may have been exempt, as favoured abbeys were after the Conquest. . . .

Apart from the witness of late monastic chroniclers which will not stand examination, the only support that Round could bring forward for his assumptions was a writ addressed to Abbot Æthelwig of Evesham, summoning to Clarendon all the knights due from all men within his bailwick and specifying in particular the five knights due from the abbot himself. There is, however, no more reason to suppose that the Conqueror had fixed the quota due from the abbot of Evesham than to suppose that he had fixed the quota due from the archbishop of Canterbury, whose service, as Anselm implies, appears to have been determined before 1066. Nor is there any reason to suppose that the secular obligations of bishops and abbots had at this early date been increased or decreased. What the obligations of other landowners were within the seven shires administered by Æthelwig we can but surmise, but to guess that they were the quotas reflected in the *servitia debita*[4] ascertained in 1166 is to guess wildly. We do not, in sober fact, know the purpose of the writ of summons; we do not know who were summoned or their numbers; we are not even certain of the year of the summons. The only certain fact, beyond those in the writ itself, is that it was issued before Æthelwig's death in 1077. It seems unlikely, however, that the purpose of the writ was to assemble the French knights who were in the service of the king's French barons. If, as is believed, the Conqueror's hold on England was precarious and "for nearly twenty years after the battle of Hastings the chances were against the survival of the Anglo-Norman monarchy" and if in 1085 King William had to bring into England an unprecedented number of French mercenaries in order to meet the threat of invasion, then it seems unlikely that the French knights resident in England, even the relatively few who could have been enfeoffed with English lands before 1077, would be permitted during Abbot Æthelwig's lifetime to stay for long quietly at home. If they constituted, as they seem to have done, an army of occupation, they were likely to be in a state of continuous mobilisation. Why it should be supposed that Æthelwig was required to summon these French knights or any of them to Clarendon is not self-evident. He seems, on the contrary, to be a most improbable agent for the purpose. And if, instead of surmising with Round that the date of the writ is 1072, we surmise that its date lies between 1067 and 1070, which seems equally possible, how then do we interpret it and what becomes of Round's thesis? We cannot build upon such flimsy foundations.

In any case, there appear to be very cogent arguments against

---

[4] Quotas of knights owed by the tenants-in-chief to the king.

the assumption that quotas of knight service were determined in 1070. Need it be recalled that Earl Waltheof was not convicted until 1076 and that his great estates could hardly have been divided among King William's French followers at any earlier date? Would it not have been extraordinary if, within four years of William's coronation, all the land in England . . . had been surveyed and newly charged with quotas of military service, with not a whisper of this tremendous operation in any contemporary chronicle, in any surviving document? And would it not have been singular, if this survey had taken place, that no trace of it should be found in the book which records the greater survey of 1086? For reasons that appear later, 1070, a year of internal strife and foreign invasion, seems a most unlucky year to pitch upon for what we venture to describe as an imaginary administrative act of major proportions. But we attach no particular significance to the year: the same objections attach to any year within Æthelwig's lifetime. The difficulty is not to find arguments against Round's assumptions but to find arguments for them. Truth to tell, his were not the usual methods of historical investigations. He scorned "the anticataclysmic tendencies of modern thought . . . the theory of gradual development and growth." His mind would not adapt itself to scientific processes. He guessed, sometimes brilliantly rightly, but as often woefully wrongly. He was at his, almost incredible, worst on this occasion.

Let us, if possible, get away from assumption and endeavour to base our conclusions upon fact. One fact stands out, that by the year 1086 the Normans were settled in England, foreign counts and barons had displaced English earls and thegns and, though there were a good many disputed titles to the lands of dispossessed English owners, the settlement was all but complete. Apart from bishoprics and abbeys, but a small minority of English owners had retained their lands and, while the estates of the churches were almost intact and had, indeed, in some cases increased, English bishops and English abbots had been replaced by foreigners. A record of the changed ownerships over the greater part of England was in course of preparation, and that record we still possess. Though it often mentions knights, it does not, however, except in the most incidental way, say anything of knight service, and we certainly cannot deduce from Domesday Book that any record of quotas of knight service had yet been made. Not only has no such record survived, but is quite certain that no record of the kind was known in the reign of Henry II. And when in 1166 it was desired to make such a record, there was no thought that quotas of knight service had been established in the eleventh century. The king's ministers did not seek to look beyond the days of the king's grandfather, Henry I. His reign was the starting-point, the period which determined the *servitium debitum:* the service a man's ancestors owed in respect of a fief in the reign of Henry I was owed in 1166. But even so, the king's ministers had no knowledge of any record made earlier in the century nor, although tenants-in-chief were required to make returns of the service due from them, does any one of them seem to have had any document to which he could refer, any charter from any king setting down the service due from any of his lands. This does not mean that there was no understanding by tenants-in-chief of their obligations, no conventional figures accepted by the exchequer upon which demands for scutage were based—the pipe rolls show that such figures, if not complete figures, existed—but, even so, there were disputes which could have been settled in the simplest possible way if there had been an authoritative record, just as disputes of another kind were settled by reference to Domesday Book. The only possible conclusion is that there was no survey and no written evidence of knight's fees in the eleventh century or at any time before 1166. . . .

If, as seems to us most probable, the neat figures of the *servitium debitum* are not as a rule historical but are arranged according to a formula, whence was this formula derived? To that question no certain answer can be given, although we can rule out Normandy which presents a very different picture in 1172, a picture which cannot have changed essentially since the days of Henry I. We cannot speak with certainty of the days of the Conqueror, for there is no written evidence; but there is no probability that the marked characteristics of knight service in the twelfth century were not already present in the duchy. In Normandy the quotas of knight service were much smaller than in England, and though there are some as high as twenty, the general run is much less. The only point in common is the recurrence of the factor of five;

but that factor is to be found just as prominently in the military obligations of hundreds and estates in pre-Conquest England. A more suggestive parallel may perhaps be drawn from the saga of Harold Fairhair, a younger contemporary of Alfred the Great, of whom it is related that, when he had conquered those parts of Norway not yet under his control, he required every earl (*jarl*) to furnish the royal army with sixty warriors and every *herse*—a rank that can be roughly equated with baron—with twenty warriors. Even if it be objected that saga history is not veridical, yet the tradition is significant, and it may be more than a coincidence that the same figure of sixty knights was the quota required from the barons to whom Henry II granted the kingdoms of Cork and Limerick.

The suggesiton we have to make is that *servitia debita*, far from having been introduced at the Conquest, were gradually established, first by the occasional settlement of disputes, as at Arundel, and thereafter by reducing those of uncertain amount to something approaching a uniform standard, beginning with ecclesiastical fiefs and culminating in the general review of 1166. This uniform standard was not derived from Norman practice, but appears to be associated with a widespread, traditional convention. The exact point on the scale at which a quota was fixed would doubtless be a matter of individual negotiation, in which the circumstances of each fief and any earlier arrangement would enter into consideration. In this way it is possible to account not only for the regular quotas (if we may so term them), but also for occasional irregularities and the quotas of fifty and twenty-five. But conjecture cannot be driven too far, and no purpose is to be served by substituting one insubstantial hypothesis for another. The points we would stress are, firstly, that the organisation of troops in multiples of five or ten was no more "feudal" than the employment of mounted soldiers in warfare, and, secondly, that there is no evidence for the general determination of *servitia debita* before the reign of Henry II and that such evidence as we have for the reign of Henry I points, not to any settled system, but to uncertainty. Above all, we would stress that no deductions regarding the size, composition, organisation or disposition of the armed forces of the Norman and Angevin kings

can be based upon the *servitia debita*, whether those convention-
ally ascribed to Henry I or those determined in 1166 which increased those conventional figures by the number of knight's
fees created since 1135. And one last word: when we speak of
the armies of this period, the one adjective we should above all
avoid is "feudal."

4   FROM   *R. R. Darlington*
                The Norman Conquest

*The excerpt below, taken from R.R. Darlington's Creighton Lecture
of 1962, published in booklet form in 1963, was written before the
appearance of Richardson's and Sayles' controversial volume. It does,
however, illustrate the self-confident defense of the "feudal revolution"
hypothesis by modern supporters of Round and Stenton. It is important to point out that in all matters other than that of feudal military service Darlington is an enthusiastic exponent of pre-Conquest
English creativity and of continuity across the line of 1066.*

The most tedious feature of some recent attempts to prove that
William I introduced nothing new is the revival of views which
have been refuted many times and the repetition of statements
which have been shown to be baseless. Apart from the more
extravagant assertions which create the impression that, in the
words of one critic, "so far from introducing feudalism after
1066 William presumably presided over its decline and fall,"[1]
the arguments are the old ones which we had thought dead, and

[1] R. S. Hoyt, review of Eric John's *Land Tenure in Early England*
(Leicester University Press, 1960), in *Speculum*, XXXVI (1961), 663–665.

SOURCE. R. R. Darlington, *The Norman Conquest*, London: The Athlone
Press, 1963, pp. 24–27. Reprinted by permission of the Athlone Press of The
University of London.

resurrection does not make them any more convincing. Even if
there were time, it would not be profitable to make a detailed
examination of the grounds on which it is once again argued that
post-Conquest military tenure developed in unbroken continuity
from Anglo-Saxon obligations. As in Maitland's day, the argument turns very largely on Worcester material, and the only new
evidence is the *Red Book of Worcester* which shows that a considerable number of knight's fees on the episcopal lands in the
twelfth century consisted of five hides. This is however of limited
significance for the evidence relating to the knight's fees of other
tenants-in-chief makes it certain that a system of five-hide fees
never existed in other parts of the country, and it has not been
proved that the five-hide fees of twelfth-century Worcester are
an Anglo-Saxon survival. The numerous charters of Bishop Oswald and his successors do not show them making grants of five
hides to their dependants, and the five-hide knight's fees of the
twelfth century which are artificially created units, comprising
pieces of land in more than one village, are quite different from
the five-hide unit of geld assessment so common in Domesday
Book, for this was a village assessed at five hides or a multiple
of five hides. Only in a limited sense was a unit of five hides
connected with Anglo-Saxon military obligations, and no satis-
factory evidence has been adduced to support the theory that
such a unit was the basis of the thegn's military service. It is surprising to find scholars maintaining that the bishop of Worcester's
quota of knights, his *servitium debitum*, was fixed before the
Conquest since this view was effectively disposed of by Round
as long ago as 1897. There is not the slightest evidence that the
bishop was bound to put sixty men in the field before the Conquest, and if he owed one knight for every five hides after the
Conquest his *servitium debitum* should have been almost double
his quota of sixty knights.[2]

2 Miss Hollings tries to surmount this difficulty by arguing from the
Red Book that neither the non-gelding hides nor the demesne land of the
bishop's manors were liable for service and arrives at figures which can be
made to fit in roughly with either the king's demand for sixty knights or
the bishop's claim that he owed only fifty. The argument is unconvincing,
for whatever may have been the principles on which the bishops of Worcester made enfeoffments after the Conquest, it is impossible to believe that so

These recent attempts to establish the Anglo-Saxon origin of the post-Conquest *servitia debita* and knight's fees must be regarded as unsuccessful. It may be doubted whether the case for continuity in military organization is helped by the contention, erroneous in my own opinion, that when we read that it was the custom to demand from a shire one soldier for a fixed number of hides and to require every hide to contribute to his expenses, the soldier in question is not a commoner but a thegn, and that the fyrd was a body of thegns. Since it is at the same time argued that the thegns are to be equated with the post-Conquest knights, the feudal host and the fyrd ought to be identical, but as a recent writer has said: "The Anglo-Norman feudal army cannot possibly have evolved out of the pre-Conquest military force because that force continued to exist for decades after the Conquest as a separate and distinct English army serving the Norman kings alongside the new feudal host."[3] Whether or not this writer is justified in claiming that the fyrd "was the primary agent through which Norman feudalism was Anglicised," its survival is proof of some measure of continuity, and in view of the important part which it played in the warfare of the first three Norman reigns, the fyrd can be described as a significant Anglo-Saxon contribution to post-Conquest military organization.

---

much of the episcopal estate was regarded by the king as exempt from military obligations either before or after the Conquest. Mr. John (*Land Tenure in Early England*), who in other respects follows very closely in the footsteps of Miss Hollings, prefers to revive Maitland's view linking the sixty knights with the triple hundred of Oswaldslaw, but like Maitland is unable to explain why the bishop did not owe service for the rest of his estates. [Mr. Darlington's footnote.]

[3] Mr. Hollister, from whose recent article on " The Norman Conquest and the Genesis of English Fudalism" (*American Historical Review*, lxvi (1961), 641–63) I have taken this sentence, rejects the view that the Anglo-Saxon army developed into the feudal host and at the same time denies that the post-Conquest military organization constituted a sudden and radical break with the past. His own "third theory which accepts Round's views on the introduction of knight service but challenges his conclusion that the effects of the Norman Conquest on English Military institutions was cataclysmic" depends largely on his views concerning the relative importance of cavalry and infantry in post-Conquest warfare which is singularly difficult to determine. [Mr. Darlington's footnote.]

5   FROM   *C. Warren Hollister*
              "1066: The 'Feudal Revolution' "

The article printed below, after summarizing the English-feudalism
controversy, concludes by finding some merit in both the "feudal
revolution" and the continuity hypotheses. The consensus which is
suggested at the end of the article may perhaps be approaching but
it has by no means arrived.

. . . Throughout the twentieth century to the present, Freeman's theory of continuity across the Thin Red Line of 1066 and
Round's theory of feudal revolution have remained the two poles
around which the controversy has ranged. English scholars of this
century have eschewed the crude political biases of their predecessors, but they have not always succeeded in avoiding a subtler
kind of bias, based on the complex antagonisms of conflicting
schools of thought, personal followings, and personal loyalties.
I do not intend to document this observation or to elaborate on
it but shall only suggest that these delicate interrelationships are
rooted firmly in the Round-Freeman controversy, and that the
biases of these two men are therefore highly relevant to us today.
Round won the battle, though perhaps not the war. His notion of
a Norman feudal revolution, asserted so boldly in the 1890's,
quickly rose to the Olympian heights of Received Opinion, and
virtually all the research done by scholars in the 1920's, 1930's
and 1940's served only to confirm and strengthen it. The most
important book on the subject written in this period, Sir Frank

SOURCE. C. Warren Hollister, "1066: The 'Feudal Revolution,' " presented
at the annual meeting of the American Historical Association, New York,
1966, and reprinted (with slight modifications) in the *American Historical
Review* Vol., LXXIII, 1968.

Stenton's *First Century of English Feudalism: 1066–1166*, incorporated Round's hypothesis in its title.

Since about mid-century, however, Round's feudal revolution hypothesis has come under attack, restrained and modest at first, but, in recent years, vigorous indeed. The past two decades or so have witnessed the emergence of a kind of "neo-Freemanism." Marjory Hollings, in 1948, urged that the Anglo-Saxon five-hide unit survived the Norman Conquest to become the basis of knights' fees in parts of the western midlands. G. O. Sayles, in 1950, argued generally for the existence of feudalism in late-Saxon England. J. O. Prestwich, in 1954, pointed to the neglected mercenary as a significant figure in Anglo-Norman warfare, thereby diminishing the military importance of the Norman feudal settlement in general and the Norman feudal knight in particular. More recently, the books of Eric John, Richardson and Sayles, and Frank Barlow, together with an accelerating flow of controversial scholarly articles in various journals, have reopened the old dispute, reviving ancient wounds and inflicting new ones, with a result that must be stimulating to some, confusing to others, and unsettling to all. At times the recently reawakened controversy has reached such levels of antagonism that we might well imagine the ghost of John Horace Round still striding fiercely along the Thin Red Line, inspiring both his supporters and opponents with his own distinctive spirit of passionate advocacy. In 1963, Richardson and Sayles could speak of Stubbs as not simply erroneous but "dogmatic and perverse," and of Round himself as "amateurish and undisciplined," "hasty and muddled," one who "fouled the wells of truth." Eric John could speak of Sir Frank Stenton as "both mistaken and inhumane," and Dorothy Whitelock could lacerate Eric John's book in a recent issue of the *American Historical Review*. . . . The debate over the feudal revolution remains not only interesting but explosive.

In an effort to bring some limited order out of the existing chaos, I would suggest that present opinion on the question of the Conquest and military service might be divided roughly into three schools of thought. First, the Round School, which includes such modern supporters of the "Feudal revolution" as Professor J. C. Holt. Second, the neo-Freeman or "direct-continuity" school represented by Richardson and Sayles, Frank Barlow, and, perhaps, Eric John. And third, a middle school to which among other historians, I would subscribe. I would call it the "Moderate School." Others less enamored of it, might prefer some adjective such as "timid" or "bland." Advocates of the moderate position will often be found contending among themselves over various points and might well resent my making schoolmates of them. Nevertheless, their views on the problem have much in common, as we shall see.

The first of these three schools, that of feudal revolution, is conveniently epitomized in Round's own words—typically lacking in self-doubt:

"I am anxious to make absolutely clear the point that between the accepted view and the view which I advance, no compromise is possible. The two are radically opposed. As against the theory that the military obligation of the Anglo-Norman tenant-in-chief was determined by the assessment of his holding, whether in hidage or value, I maintain that the extent of that obligation was not determined by his holding, but was fixed in relation to, and expressed in terms of, the *constabularia* of ten knights, the unit of the [Norman] feudal host. And I consequently hold that his military service was in no way derived or developed from that of the Anglo-Saxons but was arbitrarily fixed by the King, from whom he received his fief, irrespectively both of its size and of all pre-existent arrangements."

This view, perhaps minus the *constabularia* hypothesis, still finds strong supporters.

The contrary view is aptly summarized by Richardson and Sayles, writing some seventy years later—with equal self assurance.

"The suggestion we have to make is that the *servicia debita* [the baronial quotas to the King] far from having been introduced at the Conquest, were gradually established, first by the occasional settlement of disputes . . . and thereafter by reducing those of uncertain amount to something approaching a uniform standard, beginning with ecclesiastical fiefs and culminating in the general review of 1166 [—the royal survey of baronial enfeoffments known as the *Cartae Baronum*]. This uniform standard was not derived from Norman practice, but appears to be associated with a widespread traditional convention."

This careful statement tends to mask the potent emotions which the two authors bring to their study. Like Freeman, they admire the Anglo-Saxons—undemocratic, to be sure, but highly civilized and richly creative. Their attitude toward Normandy can only be described as one of hostility. Normandy was "a small, barbaric province" whose inhabitants "had little statecraft and little foresight . . . very little to teach and very much to learn." Thus, "The Norman Conquest introduced no new conceptions of warfare, no new ranks of society." Richardson and Sayles' intellectual debt to Freeman is perfectly clear, and the two authors recognize it explicitly: "Freeman has long been under a cloud," they write, "but it seems to us that, of all the historians during the last hundred years, he wrote the wisest words on the consequences of the Conquest."

Here are the two polar positions, uncompromisingly asserted, and each rooted firmly in the Round-Freeman controversy of the later nineteenth century. To me, and others, an intermediate position between these two extremes seems closer to reality—that the conquering Normans contributed much and preserved much, that they introduced feudal knights' service but tamed it by the Anglo-Saxon tradition of royal centralization and brought it into a larger military organization that retained significant Anglo-Saxon components.

The validity of any of these three positions depends, of course, not on how convincing it sounds in the abstract but on how well it fits the evidence. The limitations of time prohibit a thorough examination of the evidence on all points at issue, but it might be useful to touch on two specific problems that are central to the general question of revolution *versus* continuity. First, the alleged survival of the Anglo-Saxon select fryd into the Anglo-Norman period; second, the advent of knightly quotas to the king. . . . [We skip to the second problem.]

. . . Were the feudal quotas of the king's tenants-in-chief established at a blow by William the Conqueror, or did they evolve slowly and only jell in 1166 with the great feudal survey of Henry II—the *Cartae Baronum*? Here again there is a problem of evidence. We get no comprehensive data on feudal *servicia debita* until the *Cartae Baronum* and the scutage accounts in the pipe rolls of Henry II. There was no general survey of quotas during the century following the Norman Conquest. Strictly speaking, not even the *Cartae Baronum* can be so described, for it recorded enfeoffments, not quotas. All the pipe rolls prior to Henry II's reign are lost save one, and that one—the roll of 31 Henry I—does not happen to record a scutage. None of these facts demonstrate that the quotas were Angevin rather than Norman; they leave the question open, and send us on to more elusive evidence.

Before looking at examples of such evidence, one crucial point must be made. The five-hide select fyrd principle and the post-Conquest feudal-quota principle are fundamentally different. The one was a national system governed by a standardized recruitment arrangement based on the hide; the other was a system of individual, arbitrary quotas based on private contracts and on the fee. Quite apart from the evidence, the hypothesis of an evolution from the one system to the other presents very serious—perhaps insurmountable—conceptual difficulties. Mr. Eric John, arguing vigorously for the direct evolution from Anglo-Saxon hidal recruitment to Anglo-Norman feudal recruitment, makes the candid statement: "At this point I had better confess that I cannot see how this was done."

Turning to the evidence, we find once again that it is scanty, yet wherever it exists it points to the high antiquity of the 1166 quotas and, in many cases, suggests strongly that they were established by William the Conqueror. A fresh look at the evidence, in other words, suggests that Round's hypothesis concerning the Norman introduction of knights' service, narrowly conceived, still stands.

To be sure, the *Cartae Baronum* of 1166 constitute the first *comprehensive* survey of knightly enfeoffments, but there are many older records that bring the *servicia debita*, in individual cases, back to a much earlier date. There has never been any doubt that some quotas were changed slightly. Some were in dispute for generations (the bishops of Worcester argued with the monarchy for many decades as to whether they owed 50 or 60 knights). Yet the evidence is very strongly in favor of a general imposition of quotas by the Conqueror.

The point of the alleged "silence of the chroniclers" has recently been raised once again, so once again the question must be examined briefly. Excluding, for the sake of argument, the thirteenth-century St. Alban's chroniclers who place the imposition of quotas in 1070, there remain other far more nearly contemporary reports. The Abingdon Chronicle reports that as soon as the disturbances immediately following the Conquest had abated, it was noted by the king's order *how many* knights should be demanded from episcopal sees and abbeys for the defense of the realm. Abbott Athelhelm of Abingdon then granted estates to men who would hold them of the abbey and in each case stipulated the obligations that accompanied the tenures. The Ely Chronicler, writing midway through the twelfth century, probably well before the *Cartae Baronum*, stated that in 1088 King William Rufus summoned the knights according to the quotas which his father had imposed on the lands of the Church. Orderic, whose silence on the matter has been specifically and repeatedly alleged, declared that the Conqueror distributed lands to his knights in such a way that the realm should thereafter have 60,000 men to answer the royal summons. The figure of 60,000 is of course absurd—Orderic uses that particular figure repeatedly to indicate simply "a great many"—but, discounting the 60,000, we are left with the statement itself which suggests nothing less than a revolution in military tenures instituted by William the Conqueror. Thus speaks Orderic, and it would be well, once and for all, to acquit this irrepressibly loquacious man of the charge of silence.

So much for the narrative sources. What of the records? First of all, the key date is not 1166 but 1156, the date of the first good pipe-roll accounts of a scutage. The 1166 *Cartae Baronum* themselves contain comprehensive testimony to enfeoffments not only in 1166 but also in 1135, and show that enfeoffments changed only slightly between these two dates. Thus, the 1166 quotas are, by implication, carried back to 1135. And in individual cases we can carry them back much further. Fixed quotas appear in the Norman Bayeux Inquest of 1133 which almost surely attests to conditions on the Bayeux estates around 1100.

Records relating to particular fiefs sometimes enable us to carry back the 1166 quotas into the reign of the Conqueror. Anyone who is inclined to question the hypothesis that the feudal quotas were established by William the Conqueror should first look closely at the records of such estates as Evesham, Peterborough, and Abingdon. Evesham possessed estates totaling some 160 hides, many of them in Worcestershire, a county wherein the 300-hide Anglo-Saxon ship sokes have been clearly traced and in which, therefore, the related five-hide rule surely obtained. At the rate of one man from every five hides, Evesham's 160 hides would yield a quota of 32 men to the Anglo-Saxon select fyrd. But the invaluable military summons of William the Conqueror to Abbot Aethelwig of Evesham of about 1072 alludes to a quota of only five men. We know, from a charter of Henry I and from later pipe-roll evidence, that Evesham's feudal quota wavered a bit, from 4½ knights to 5 knights, but at no time did the knightly quota approach the select-fyrd quota of, presumably, 32 warriors. It was 5 knights in 1166; it was 5 knights in 1072.

At Peterborough the fyrd quota is exceedingly difficult to determine because of a widespread and irregular incidence of beneficial hidation combined with the fact that many Peterborough estates were assessed in geld carucates rather than hides. The best figure I can give for the Peterborough fyrd quota is 70—and this is decidedly tentative. The feudal *servicium* in Henry II's pipe rolls is 60, with 64 fees existing on the estates in both 1166 and 1135. Of these 64 fees, 62 are described by Walter of Whittlesey and John of Peterborough as having been created by Abbot Turold in about 1070. The feudal quota of 60 is very high considering the size of the Peterborough estates, and, in consequence, the individual Peterborough knights' fees are singularly small. It seems most likely that the 60-knight *servicium debitum* was a punative quota imposed by the Conqueror in reply to the support given by Peterborough tenants to Hereward's rebellion. Indeed, Hereward himself appears to have been a Peterborough tenant.

Abingdon held some 624½ hides in 1066, chiefly in Berkshire—where the five-hide rule is unquestioned—with some land in Oxfordshire and a little in Gloucestershire. The assessment of 624½ hides in 1066 was reduced by 1086 to 425¾. Dividing these figures by five, we get five-hide fyrd quotas of about 125 men in 1066 dropping to about 85 men in 1086. But a knight list of William the Conqueror's time in the *Abingdon Chronicle* discloses only 31 fees. The same chronicle reports that nearly all the Abingdon knights were required to join King William's Welsh campaign of 1081, and we might reasonably conclude that on this occasion Abingdon must have sent some 30 knights or so to the royal summons. An almost identical number—33 fees—is disclosed in the *Carta* of 1166, and Henry II's pipe rolls attest to a feudal quota of 30 knights. Thus once again the enfeoffments of the Conqueror's time, utterly unrelated to the fyrd quota, are tightly correlated to the feudal quota as it emerges in Henry II's pipe rolls.

Professor Robert S. Hoyt, incidentally, has observed in an unpublished paper that at Abingdon the double burden on the land—of five-hide quota and feudal quota—is more than balanced by the Conqueror's reduction in hidage. In 1066, at one man per five hides, Abingdon owed 125 men to the select fyrd. In 1086, with the reduced hidage assessment, the same Abingdon estates owed 85 men to the select fyrd plus 30 knights to the feudal host, or a total of 115 men to both forces. In short, the single obligation in 1066 required 125 men; the double obligation of 1086 required 115 men. It must be added that other fiefs do not yield such tidy results, but it remains a possibility that there may be some significant connection between the Conqueror's uncharacteristically generous policy of widespread beneficial hidation and the establishment of a twofold military obligation on the land.

Notice that the quotas of Evesham, Peterborough, and Abingdon—5 knights, 60, and 30—are all divisible by five. In this respect they are characteristic of the feudal quotas in general. The *Cartae Baronum* and Henry II's pipe rolls disclose a strikingly symmetrical system of round quotas. There are some exceptions to this rule, but the tendency is strong and unmistakable. Quotas of 5 knights, 10, 20, 40, 60, and so on, occur repeatedly. John Horace Round associated these figures with his hypothetical 10-knight constabularies. He was doubtless mistaken, yet clearly they suggest the work of a single authoritative assessor. If one can be forgiven for applying a hoary theological argument to this very mundane problem, it may be said that such remarkable symmetry as we find in the English feudal quotas cannot have been the accidental result of individual bargains hammered out over the decades, nor can it have arisen from the older five-hide recruitment system. For if we calculate the hides of the tenants-in-chief and divide by five, the resulting quotas are not round but bewilderingly miscellaneous. A single assessor was evidently responsible for this coherent structure of feudal quotas, and in the light of all the evidence, we can confidently identify the assessor as William the Conqueror.

The Round hypothesis, that the English feudal quotas were established by the Conqueror, has traditionally carried the corollary that William brought the feudal quota system into England from Normandy. Round assumed this without serious investigation, and his assumption was apparently confirmed early in the present century by Charles Homer Haskins.[1] Although Haskins' sources dated for the most part from the post-Conquest period, and largely from the twelfth century, he nevertheless argued persuasively that a coherent and encompassing system of feudal quotas existed in pre-Conquest Normandy and, indeed, served as William's model. Such a conclusion seemed unarguable, for if the Anglo-Norman *servicia debita* were introduced by the Conqueror, and if they had no Anglo-Saxon roots, where else might they have come from than Normandy?

More recently, however, Haskins' conclusion has been effectively qualified in the writings of David Douglas, Lucien Musset, and Joseph R. Strayer. As Professor Strayer has pointed out, fixed quotas are conspicuously absent in enfeoffment charters issued by dukes of Normandy prior to the Conquest. And although such quotas may have been developing, at least on Norman ecclesiastical estates, on the eve of 1066, they appear to have been not only far lower but also much less comprehensive than those imposed by the Conqueror on the estates of post-Conquest England. In short, the feudal quota system of William the Conqueror's England was not a purely Norman importation. Rather it was a bold extrapolation of limited and undeveloped Norman precedents, greatly expanded and systematized by the Conqueror as he exploited the vast opportunities afforded by his power over a conquered land. It is possible, therefore, to speak not only of the Norman impact on the development of English feudalism but also

[1] *Norman Institutions* (Cambridge, Mass., 1918.).

of the English impact on the development of Norman feudalism. The key word is not "importation" but "interaction." "It may be," writes Strayer, "that Normandy was made to conform to the English model, rather than the reverse." Or, as Douglas has put it, "If English feudalism was essentially Norman, so also was Norman feudalism by the end of the eleventh century, in some sense, English."

Such, then, are the implications of some of the evidence regarding certain crucial issues of the Norman Conquest. There are many other issues, and the diverse interpretations of various historians are apt to convey the impression of confusion and chaos. But despite this appearance, we can detect a broad consensus developing in the independent and often concurrent investigations of a great many modern scholars of the Conquest. Agreement is assuredly not complete; far from it! Yet as we examine the works of such men as Michael Powicke, J. O. Prestwich, R. C. Smail, John Beeler, David Douglas (in his *William the Conqueror*), and others, we can see, beneath the surface controversy, a general consensus with varying emphases. All agree that the *servicia debita* were imposed by the Conqueror, that they represent an institutional break from the Anglo-Saxon past, that there were, nevertheless, important elements of institutional continuity between the military organizations of Saxon and Norman England, and that the first century of English feudalism was not so feudal as has sometimes been thought. Sir Frank Stenton himself, of course, was by no means insensitive to the continuity of institutions across the line of 1066. R. C. Smail has written:

"Even from the late-eleventh century, when English feudal institutions were still in process of formation, the Conqueror and his sons after him relied on non-feudal sources of recruitment. It is doubtful whether the military needs of the English kings could ever have been met from feudal sources alone."

Michael Powicke, in his fine book on military obligation in medieval England, stresses at once the importance and the limitations of William I's new feudal army, and gives due attention to the Anglo-Norman mercenaries and the English. John Beeler, in his articles and in his illuminating new book on English medieval warfare, puts slightly greater stress on the service of the knightly feudal contingents, but presents the same heterogeneous picture of the Anglo-Norman army and makes the same distinction between fyrd and feudal host. J. O. Prestwich, although hostile to the renewed emphasis on institutional continuity, has himself recently suggested an important and previously neglected example of it in the military households of the Saxon and Norman Kings, which constituted the cores of pre- and post-Conquest English armies. I am a little worried about his overly exact translation of *familia* as "household," but Prestwich is nevertheless basically correct and has made a significant point. David Douglas has written recently, "The successful imposition of tenure by service upon his magnates in respect of their English lands must be regarded as one of the most notable of the Conqueror's achievements." But he also states that "The Norman impact upon England was to be drastically modified by English tradition under the direction of the Norman King." And Douglas emphasizes the Conqueror's use of the five-hide fyrd and mercenaries. Here, in a nutshell, is the fundamental position which, I believe, is coming more and more to be accepted.

It is good to have controversy, but it is good, also, to find that the majority of investigators are not looking at the problem in totally diverse ways, to find some reason for believing that, as our knowledge grows, there is developing the tendency for dispassionate scholars to agree on certain fundamental points. And at the moment I am optimistic as regards the problem of the Norman Conquest.

PART FIVE

Summary

1 FROM R. H. C. Davis
"The Norman Conquest"

Mr. R.H.C. Davis, fellow of Merton College, Oxford, presents here a thoughtful and broadly conceived interpretation of the Conquest, arguing that the success of the conquerors was, ironically, a direct consequence of the political precocity of their Anglo-Saxon predecessors.

The most interesting problem about the Norman Conquest is what made it so complete. If it were not such a familiar fact, we would have thought it incredible that England, or any other state, could have been completely overwhelmed after a single battle. But this was what happened after the Battle of Hastings. Apparently as the result of one day's fighting (14 October 1066), England received a new royal dynasty, a new aristocracy, a virtually new Church, a new art, a new architecture and a new language. By 1086, when Domesday Book was made, less than half-a-dozen of the 180 greater land-lords or tenants-in-chief were English. By 1090 only one of the 16 English bishoprics was held by an Englishman, and six of the sees had been moved from their historic centres to large towns. By the end of the twelfth century almost every Anglo-Saxon cathedral and abbey had been pulled down and rebuilt in the Norman style. Nothing was allowed to stand which might remind the English of the glories of their past. The Normans put it out that the Anglo-Saxons had been used to wooden palaces and wooden churches, that they had lived by a "natural" economy, and that since they had no money they had been forced to pay their taxes in kind. They claimed that their military prowess had been ineffectual and their culture non-existent, and they relegated the English language to the underworld of the lower classes. For almost two centuries the language

SOURCE. R. H. C. Davis, "The Norman Conquest," *History*, Vol. LI, 1966, pp. 279–286. Reprinted by permission of *History* and the author.

of polite society—the aristocracy and the court—was French, and
the reality of the Engilsh past was smothered with romantic
stories about King Arthur and the ancient Britons.

To some extent the explanation of these facts must be sought
in the larger European background. The third quarter of the
eleventh century was a period of rapid development throughout
Western Europe, and it was possible for countries which suffered
no Norman conquest to be transformed in some of the same ways
as England. The reform of the Church, for example, was a general
movement which swept across Europe in the 1050s and 1060s,
and would presumably have reached England in any case by the
time of Pope Gregory VII (1073-85). Economic prosperity was
increasing everywhere, as evidenced particularly by the spec-
tacular expansion of the Flemish cloth industry, for which England supplied most of the raw wool. Churches and palaces were
being built or enlarged in the new Romanesque style throughout
Latin Christendom. What was particular to the Normans was the
skill with which they exploited these movements. They reformed
the English Church in such a way that it became less English and
more Norman, and they developed an advanced type of Romanesque architecture because the conquest of England had made
them so rich that there was almost no limit to the number or size
of their buildings.[1] Above all they succeeded in expropriating all
the greater English landlords, so that they could step into their
shoes as a new Norman aristocracy. In sharp contrast to the
English plantations of Ireland or the more recent efforts of
colonial powers in Africa and Asia, the Norman settlement of
England was completed in less than twenty years and has been
accepted as a "natural" fact of English history for nine centuries.
By what means was it accomplished?

Perhaps the most obvious reason for the success of the Norman
settlement was that William had a legitimate claim to the English
crown. After the death of Harold, the only possible alternative was
the aetheling Edgar, and since he was too young and too much of

---

[1] It is sometimes forgotten that most of the Romanesque churches of
Normandy were built *after* the conquest of England. The only notable exceptions are Bernay (*c.* 1017–50), the nave of Mont Saint-Michel (*c.* 1040)
and Jumièges (1040–67), and the chancel of the Abbaye aux Dames at Caen
(1062–6). [Mr. Davis' footnote.]

a simpleton to inspire confidence, the English had no option but to accept William as their king. But his accession would have had little practical effect if it had not been for the fact that the English kingdom had an efficient system of government. Countries which are well governed should be able to resist invading armies more easily than countries which are not, but if by any chance they fail they are easier for a conqueror to control. They do not lend themselves to guerrilla resistance, because efficient governments remove the opportunities for such activities.

It was therefore important that the English administrative machine was probably the most efficient in the whole of Western Europe. Its strength lay in the fact that it had trained officials in charge of both central and local administration. There was a royal exchequer which received taxes, a chancery (or writing office) which produced standardized letters (writs) to convey instructions to the provinces, and local officials who had been trained to obey them. The most important of these officials were the shire-reeves or sheriffs who, as their name implied, controlled the shires. In contrast to the local divisions of France, Normandy, or most other parts of Europe, the English shires covered the whole kingdom and had boundaries which were well-known and precisely defined. There was no vagueness about what belonged to where, and as a result it was difficult, if not impossible, for any person or place to evade the control of the sheriff. Every village belonged to a "hundred" which had a court every four weeks, and every "hundred" belonged to a shire which twice a year held a court which all the principal men were compelled to attend. Their meetings provided an occasion not only for giving judgements in lawsuits, but also for receiving the orders of the king.

Two examples may be given to show the enormous power which these institutions gave to an English King. First they enabled him to levy a land-tax on the whole kingdom at regular intervals. The tax was called *geld*, and it was levied at the rate of so many shillings (usually two) on the "hide." The whole of England was divided into hides or carucates—taxable units of a notional value and usually something like 120 acres in size—and the central government knew how many hides there were deemed to be in every shire. The demand for the tax was sent to the shire

court which divided it among its component "hundreds"; in the
hundred courts it was subdivided among the component tithings;
and within each tithing each landholder knew what proportion
he had to pay. When, in the tenth century, Anglo-Saxon kings
had declared that every man had to be in a hundred and tithing,
they were ensuring not only that all men could be brought to
justice but also that they could be taxed. As a system it was unique
in Western Europe, and we can well imagine that William the
Conqueror was both amazed and delighted, when he discovered
that by merely declaring a geld year he would receive cartloads
of money with no further effort of his own.

The second example of governmental power concerns the coinage in which the tax was collected. Not only were all moneyers
appointed by the crown, but (in the words of a recent authority)
"they were dependent for their dies on a strictly-controlled die-
cutting agency, and each man's name was stamped on his work."
From 973 to 1066, and even later, the coin-types were apparently
changed at six-yearly intervals, when all money had to be brought
in and re-minted. So as to facilitate this re-minting there were at
least 40, and perhaps as many as 70 minting-places in England, so
distributed that hardly a village south of the Trent would have
been more than 15 miles from one of them. The succeeding types
of coin could, and did, vary in weight, and it has been claimed
that these variations amounted to a systematic monetary policy.
To quote the numismatists again, "such elaborate control of the
coinage was almost unprecedented in a medieval state; one would
probably have to look as far as the Byzantine empire to find a
more complex monetary policy," a fine contrast to the Norman
stories about the Anglo-Saxons having to pay their taxes in kind!

The government which fell into the hands of the Conqueror
was efficient and centralized, and William realized its potentialities
at once. Though it had been devised to provide England with an
army for its defence, it could now be used as an instrument of
expropriation, so that the lands of the English could be trans-
ferred to Norman ownership. It was for this reason that William
was anxious to stress his rights as the lawful heir of Edward the
Confessor; he had to preserve the continuity of the Anglo-Saxon
administrative system in order to make his conquest complete.
He welcomed the continued service of Anglo-Saxon scribes in

his chancery, Anglo-Saxon sheriffs and portreeves in shires and boroughs, an Anglo-Saxon justiciar in the six West Midland shires, three Anglo-Saxon earls, and the Anglo-Saxon archbishop of Canterbury. He might not need their services for long, but he needed them urgently until sufficient Normans or other foreigners had been trained to replace them.

In order to secure the collaboration of these men, William would have had to make them believe that what he wanted was a "genuine Anglo-Norman state," in which equal protection would be given to all men, whether English or Norman. To Englishmen of the time the notion would not have seemed implausible, because the last conquest which they had experienced, only 50 years before, had been that of King Cnut who had pursued just such a policy and had become almost more English than the English. For William, however, such an Anglophile policy can never have been more than wishful-thinking, if as much as that. He had recruited his army not only from Normandy, but also from northern France, Brittany and Flanders, and (as has often been observed) it was something like a joint-stock enterprise. Those who took part in it not only expected to be rewarded with land in England, but required it; and it was obviously impossible to satisfy them without expropriating large numbers of Englishmen.

We have very little information about the way in which the land was allotted to the leading Normans, but the subject is an important one and deserves investigation. We know that William had made some grants of land before he returned to Normandy in February 1067, but by then he could have known little more of England than what he had been able to see on his march from Hastings to London by way of Wallingford and Berkhamsted. It must therefore have been difficult for him to know what land he had at his disposal. English collaborators, such as the earls Edwin, Morcar and Waltheof, may have given him information about the men who had fought against him at Senlac, so that a start could be made with the distribution of their lands; but even so, William can hardly have known the exact location or extent of the estates concerned. That, presumably, was why he had to extemporize by granting to individual Normans the lands which had been held by particular Anglo-Saxons in specified

shires. It would not have mattered if he did not know precisely
what those lands were, provided he had a rough idea of their
value; but sometimes he seems to have made mistakes, rewarding
some men more lavishly and others more meagrely than he had
intended. Orderic Vitalis tells us that while some Normans found
themselves endowed with lands which were rich beyond expecta-
tion, others complained that they had been given "barren farms
and domains depopulated by war."

It therefore looks as if a Norman who was granted the lands
of a particular Anglo-Saxon was expected to discover for himself
exactly what and where those lands were. The task must have
seemed formidable. A Norman could not very well ride round
an English shire "alone and palely loitering" asking in every village
if Ulf or Tovi had held any land there; even if the villagers had
been able to understand him, they would probably have done their
best to cheat him, if not to murder him. To the Normans, therefore, it must have seemed a godsend that the Anglo-Saxon administrative machine provided an easy way of getting the necessary
information. The procedure was that anyone who was granted
land by the king was given a sealed writ which stated the fact
and had to be taken to the relevant shire court to be inspected
and read out aloud. The theory was that the whole shire was thus
made witness of the king's grant, and would be held responsible
for its execution; in this case it would have to inform the Norman
what the lands of his predecessor were, and help him gain possession of them.

In the circumstances of the Conquest, it might well have been
feared that the theory would not be strictly observed, and that
King William's writ would be received with less respect than
that of King Edward the Confessor. Even so, it must have been
a great help for the Normans to know that all the landholders of
a shire would be assembled at the shire-court at six-monthly intervals. The meeting-place would be known—it was usually in the
open air and away from towns—and it would not have been
difficult for a body of Normans to arrive with a strong force of
soldiers and surround the place completely. With no escape
possible, the members (or "suitors") of the court could soon have
been reduced to a state of terror, so that the Normans could
present their writs and demand the necessary information and

assistance. Since William the Conqueror was careful not to expropriate all the English at once, there would probably have been some who were willing to be coerced, in the hope that they would be able to save their own property by giving information about that of their neighbours. Failing such collaboration it would have been necessary to use violence, but if the Normans were in sufficient force, and the court effectively surrounded, any attempt to refuse the information would have been suicidal, unless it took the form of planned rebellion. Rebellions did in fact occur in some shires in 1067, but they were not concerted, because William had removed all the natural leaders and taken them with him to Normandy. When he returned to England at the end of the year, he suppressed the revolts with ease, and made them the excuse for further expropriations.

Even in shires where there were no rebellions, it would have been some time before it was safe for the Normans to split up and reside on their new estates, for if they had dispersed immediately, it would have been easy for the English to murder them in their beds. For some years the Normans would have had no option but to behave in the manner of all armies of occupation, living, eating and sleeping together in operational units. We know that they built castles in the chief towns of nearly all shires, and we may assume that they lived in them as the "household knights" of their overlords, exploiting their estates as absentee landlords for the time being. How they managed it we do not know, but if we may make a guess, it would be that they toured the whole shire in force, and interrogated the men of each village with brutality, until they had been told what dues their predecessors had received from their respective estates. If they did not think their predecessors had received enough, they could doubtless have demanded more; and they would probably have threatened to burn the village or kill its inhabitants, if the full amount were not brought to the castle by the stipulated date. The Normans proved themselves capable of such conduct in the Harrying of the North.

Castles were by far the most important instrument which the Normans used for the subjugation of the country. Before the Conquest they had been almost unknown in England, for they were basically different from the fortified towns or boroughs of the Anglo-Saxons. The boroughs were large because they had been designed as places where all men could take refuge against external invaders. The castle, on the other hand, was small and was designed as a place from which a few men could dominate a subject population. Basically it was a wooden tower erected on a mound of earth (or *motte*), the purpose of which was to defend the base of the tower from incendiaries, while also being steep enough to make a cavalry-charge impossible. Though small in comparison to a borough, the building of a *motte* must have been a major undertaking. The one at Oxford was 64 ft. high with a diameter of 81 ft. at the top and 250 ft. at the base; it consisted of more than a million-and-a-half cubic feet of earth, all of which would have been piled up by the forced labour of the townsmen, working with spades, baskets and wheelbarrows. The site of Oxford's *motte* was typical, since it was not in the centre of the old borough where the townsmen could have surrounded it, but at one extremity where the Norman garrison could keep in touch with the outside world if the town was in revolt. It had been designed as an instrument of oppression and was undoubtedly effective; in the opinion of Orderic Vitalis the English would never have been conquered if they had possessed castles of their own.

In the general confusion and terror of the Conquest, there must have been many opportunities for individual Normans to seize more lands than they had been granted, and the *clamores* of Domesday Book[2] show that it was by no means uncommon for one Norman to take possession of a manor which should have gone to another. In some cases this seems to have been done with no attempt to conceal the use of naked force in a cloak of legality, but in others the Normans concerned attempted to secure their position by forcing the shire court to give false evidence. In many cases they may have succeeded in covering their traces completely, but we know of some in which they failed. Rochester cathedral has preserved a full account of the way in which a Norman sheriff, Picot, attempted to rob it of its manor at Frecken-ham (Suff.) by claiming it as royal demesne and keeping the

[2] A section of Domesday Book devoted to disputes over lands and obligations.

profits himself. So long as the bishop was only an Anglo-Saxon, the sheriff experienced no difficulty, but after 1076 there was a Norman bishop of Rochester, and he immediately complained to the king.

"The king ordered all the men of the county to be assembled, so that it might be proved by their judgment whose the land ought to be. The men were assembled, and from fear of the sheriff affirmed, that the land was not St. Andrew's [of Rochester] but the king's. Since the bishop of Bayeux, who was presiding over the plea, did not put much faith in them, he ordered them, if they knew that what they said was true, to choose twelve of their number to confirm on oath what they had all said. But they, when they had withdrawn for consultation, were terrified by a message from the sheriff, and swore that what they had said was true."[3]

There the matter might have rested, if the Norman bishop of Rochester had not at last discovered the Anglo-Saxon monk who had previously managed the estate for the cathedral. In the face of his evidence one of the jurors was forced to admit that he had committed perjury. Rochester recovered its land, and the twelve jurors were fined £300, an enormous sum for a time when £20 a year was considered a suitable income for a Norman knight. It was necessary to be severe "pour encourager les autres," for the only way in which the king could prevent his followers from helping themselves to all the lands they wished, was by ensuring that the shire courts did not turn a blind eye to their activities.

Eventually the Conqueror extended his inquiries to the whole kingdom, in order to produce the Domesday Survey (1086). Commissioners went round all the shire courts and inquired into all the possessions of the king, the churches and all the magnates, enumerating the number of hides or carucates, the amount of plough-land, wood, meadow, sokemen, villeins, serfs and cattle, and estimating the value of each estate at three different dates— when King Edward was alive (1065), when its present holder first took possession, and as it actually was in 1086. In this way William used the basic machinery of the Anglo-Saxon govern-

[3] *Registrum Roffense*, ed. J. Thorpe (London, 1769), p. 31. [Mr. Davis' footnote].

ment, in order to discover the exact location, extent, and value
of the lands which he had given his followers. He was also able
to detect if they had seized more lands than they had been
granted, for the first question asked about each manor was "Who
held it in King Edward's time?" and if the answer was not the
present holder's official *antecessor*,[4] there would be trouble in
store. At Wilksby in the South Riding of Lindsey the commissioners reported on a claim by the bishop of Durham against
Gilbert de Gant, declaring that "the men of the Riding say they
never saw the bishop's *antecessor* given seisin either by writ or
by envoy (*legatum*), and they give their testimony in favour of
Gilbert" (i.375). In cases where the royal demesne had suffered,
their language became more threatening:—"Berengar the vassal of
St. Edmund's (Abbey) 'invaded' this, and is in the king's mercy.
He was ill and could not come to the hearing." (ii. 449).

The Domesday Survey brought the Norman Conquest to a
conclusion by examining all the details of the ruthless spoliation,
and approving them only when they had been done by authority.
That was how it got its name; it was the survey and book of
Judgement Day. Every Norman had been forced to account for
the way in which he had acquired his English lands; and if it
was approved, his name was inscribed and his claim upheld for
ever by the hundred, the shire, the king's justices and the king.
It brought the tenurial revolution to an end and made the Norman settlement permanent.

It is a commonplace of history that the difficulties of getting
a revolution started are nothing like so great as those of getting
it to stop. The men who first put it in motion are usually swept
away by those who follow, and the passage from one change to
the next becomes increasingly rapid as the revolution gathers mo-
mentum. That something of this sort nearly happened after the
Norman Conquest, is suggested by the fact that some lands had
changed hands two or three times between 1066 and 1086, but
William the Conqueror did not lose control of the situation.
His grip was firm, because he recognized the potentiality of the

---

[4] His officially-designated Anglo-Saxon predecessor in the holding of the
land in question.

Anglo-Saxon machinery of government and exploited it to the full. He used it to expropriate the English and to make the Domesday Survey, to start his revolution and to bring it to a halt. And in so doing he demonstrated to the English what a formidable weapon their kings had devised for their undoing.

CONCLUSION

Implicit in the problem of the Norman Conquest are a series of deeper issues which relate to sociology and the philosophy of history. Is it possible to frame generalizations which illuminate historical conquests in general? The same problems of the relations of conquerors to conquered arise repeatedly in world history —in the several conquests of China, the Roman conquests of Gaul and the Hellenistic world, the Germanic conquests of Rome, the Islamic conquests of Syria, Persia, and North Africa, and, more immediately relevant, the Norman conquest of southern Italy and Sicily, the conquest of the Holy Land by the crusaders, and the Danish conquest of Anglo-Saxon England. Do the conquerors transform the subject culture, are they transformed by it, or do they, at the same time, draw from it and contribute to it? The answer depends, in individual instances, on several variables: the relative sophistication and vitality of the two cultures involved, the extent of new settlement by the conquerors in the conquered land, the social level of the new settlers. The Danish conquests of England brought in large numbers of Scandinavian peasant-farmers whose settlement deeply affected agrarian institutions in northern and eastern England. The Norman settlers, on the other hand, were chiefly members of the warrior aristocracy, with the result that the Norman Conquest controversy centers around the questions of feudalism and military institutions. In other areas, English institutions and culture evolved gradually. Their rapid growth in the post-Conquest era resulted largely from the pan-European twelfth-century renaissance and the intensification of European vitality and inventiveness which we associate with the coming of the High Middle Ages.

On the interlocked issues of feudalism and military institutions, historians continue to disagree. Sufficient material has been included here to permit the reader to gain an impression of some of the issues involved and a sampling of the historical evidence. The reader is urged to be particularly skeptical of the editor's own views on the subject, for in his combined role of editor and contributor he may well be stacking the deck. Let the reader beware! Let him read further if possible, reason the issues out for himself, apply his own critical intellect to these problems, wrestle with the evidence, and arrive at conclusions that are neither those of Stubbs or Richardson and Sayles, Freeman or Round, Stenton, Eric John or Hollister, but his own.

SUGGESTIONS FOR FURTHER READING

GENERAL WORKS ON THE NORMAN CONQUEST

A scholarly account of the Norman Conquest and its implications will be found in Sir Frank Stenton, *Anglo-Saxon England* (2nd ed., Oxford, 1947), pp. 537-678. For a more elementary treatment see C. Warren Hollister, *The Making of England* (Boston, 1966), pp. 59-120.

The Norman Conquest was analyzed by a number of distinguished English scholars of the later nineteenth and early twentieth centuries. Among the most notable of their works are William Stubbs, *The Constitutional History of England* I, (6th ed., Oxford, 1897), especially pp. 183-355; Edward A. Freeman, *The History of the Norman Conquest of England* (6 vols., Oxford, 1867-79), especially V, 333-651; F. W. Maitland, *Domesday Book and Beyond* (Cambridge, Eng., 1897; reprinted in paperback, London, 1960); and Paul Vinogradoff, *English Society in the Eleventh Century* (Oxford, 1908). For the Norman background see C. H. Haskins, *Norman Institutions* (Cambridge, Mass., 1918), and, more recently, David Douglas, *William the Conqueror: The Norman Impact upon England* (London, 1964); Douglas' sections on Normandy (pp. 1-180) are especially illuminating, but the whole of this excellent biography should be read. Another fine study of the Conqueror, far shorter, is Frank Barlow, *William I and the Norman Conquest* (London, 1965). The historiography of the Conquest is skillfully presented in David Douglas, *The Norman Conquest and British Historians* (Glasgow, 1946).

The decade of the 1960's has been particularly rich in volumes on the Conquest, and 1966, the year of the ninth centenary, yielded an avalanche of them. Among the more useful of these are R. R. Darlington, *The Norman Conquest* (London, 1963)—a sympathetic defense of Anglo-Saxon culture; Henry Loyn, *The Norman Conquest* (London, 1965)—a brief, lucid summary—and, by the same author *Anglo-Saxon England and the Norman Conquest* (Oxford, 1962)—a longer work stressing economic and social history, of which pp. 315-384 are the most relevant to the Conquest. Of the centenary books, the most useful and authoritative is *The Norman Conquest: Its Setting and Impact*, edited by C. T. Chevallier (London, 1966), which includes four essays written on a nontechnical level by four excellent scholars: Dorothy Whitelock, David Douglas, Charles H. Lemmon, and Frank Barlow. The most provocative recent book on the subject, by all odds, is H. G. Richardson and G. O. Sayles, *The Governance of Mediaeval England from the Conquest to Magna Carta* (Edinburgh, 1963), especially pp. 1-135.

An extensive collection of translated original sources of the period is *English Historical Documents*, II, *1042–1189,* edited by David Douglas and G. W. Greenaway (London, 1953). The *Anglo-Saxon Chronicle* has been well translated by G. N. Garmonsway (London and New York, 1953), and by Dorothy Whitelock, David Douglas, and Susie I. Tucker (London, 1961), the latter translation being based on translations in *English Historical Documents* (above), which also contains translated excerpts from other contemporary chronicles.

SPECIAL TOPICS

For differing interpretations of the Conquest's implications in the field of law see Doris M. Stenton, *English Justice between the Norman Conquest and the Great Charter, 1066–1215* (Philadelphia, 1964); H. G. Richardson and G. O. Sayles, *Law and Legislation in England from Aethelbert to Magna Carta* (Edinburgh, 1966), especially pp. 30-53; and George W. Keeton, *The Norman Conquest and the Common Law* (London, 1966). The effect of the Conquest on English urban institutions, once a matter of controversy, was effectively settled by James Tait, *The Medieval English Borough* (Manchester, 1936). An excellent analysis of post-Conquest agrarian history is Reginald Lennard, *Rural England, 1086–1135: A Study of Social and Agrarian Conditions* (Oxford, 1959).

A thoughtful discussion of the Conquest's effect on the English Church will be found in Dom David Knowles, *The Monastic Order in England* (Cambridge, Engl., 1950), pp. 100-144. One should also consult Norman Cantor's provocative work, *Church, Kingship, and Lay Investiture in England, 1089–1135* (Princeton, 1958). Two original sources (now in English translation) which illuminate the post-Conquest Church are *The Monastic Constitutions of Lanfranc*, edited by Dom David Knowles (Nelson's Medieval Texts, London, 1951), and Hugh the Chantor, *The History of the Church of York, 1066–1127*, edited by Charles Johnson (Nelson's Medieval Texts, London, 1961).

THE QUESTION OF FEUDALISM

The starting point for modern research on the problem is John Horace Round, *Feudal England* (London, 1895), and especially the essay in the book entitled "The Introduction of Knight Service into England" (pp. 225-314). Two important studies, both published in 1932, cast a great deal of new light on the problem without differing fundamentally from Round: Sir Frank Stenton, *The First Century of English Feudalism, 1066–1166* (Oxford, 1932; 2nd ed., 1961); and Helena M. Chew, *The English Ecclesiastical Tenants-in-Chief and Knight Service* (Oxford, 1932). The general problem and its historiography are discussed in scholarly articles by David Douglas, "The Norman Conquest and English Feudalism," *Economic History Review*, IX (1939), 128–143; Carl Stephenson, "Feudalism and Its Antecedents in England," *American Historical Review*, XLVIII (1943), 245–265; and C. Warren Hollister, "The Norman Conquest and the Genesis of English Feudalism," *American Historical Review*, LXVI (1961), 641-663. Important discussions of English feudalism and the Conquest will be found in several books already cited above under "General Works on the Norman Conquest." See particularly the works of Freeman, Maitland, Vinogradoff, Douglas, Haskins, and Richardson and Sayles (pp. 42-91).

The more recent books bearing directly on the subject are M. R. Powicke, *Military Obligation in Medieval England* (Oxford, 1962), especially pp. 1-47; C. Warren Hollister, *Anglo-Saxon Military Institutions* (Oxford, 1962), and *The Military Organization of Norman England* (Oxford, 1965); Eric John,

Land Tenure in Early England (Leicester, 1960), pp. 113-161, and *Orbis Britanniae* (Leicester, 1966), pp. 128–153; and John Beeler, *Warfare in England, 1066–1189* (Ithaca, N.Y., 1966). The establishment and growth of an important Norman noble family in England is deftly traced in W. E. Wightman, *The Lacy Family in England and Normandy, 1066–1194* (Oxford, 1966).

A significant article demonstrating the importance of mercenaries *vis-à-vis* feudal knights in the immediate post-Conquest era is J. O. Prestwich, "War and Finance in the Anglo-Norman State," *Transactions of the Royal Historical Society*, 5th series, IV (1954), 19-43. Anyone wishing to examine additional recent technical arguments on the subject of feudalism and the Conquest is directed to the following articles: Marjory Hollings, "The Survival of the Five-Hide Unit in the Western Midlands," *English Historical Review*, LXIII (1948), 453–487; John Beeler, "The Composition of Anglo-Norman Armies," *Speculum*, XL (1965), 398-414; J. O. Prestwich, "Anglo-Norman Feudalism and the Problem of Continuity," *Past and Present*, XXVI (1963), 39-57; C. Warren Hollister, "The Significance of Scutage Rates," *English Historical Review*, LXXV (1960), 577-588; J. C. Holt, "Feudalism Revisited," *Economic History Review*, 2nd series, XIV (1961), 333-340; and J. C. Holt and C. Warren Hollister, "Two Comments on the Problem of Continuity in Anglo-Norman Feudalism," *Economic History Review*, 2nd series, XVI (1963), 104-118. A particularly controversial problem is thoroughly ironed out in the following sequence of articles: C. Warren Hollister, "The Irony of English Feudalism," *Journal of British Studies*, II, ii (1963), 1-26; Robert S. Hoyt, "The Iron Age of English Feudalism," *ibid.*, II, ii (1963), 27-30; C. Warren Hollister, "The Irony of the Iron Age," *ibid.*, II, ii (1963), 31-32; Fredric L. Cheyette, "Some Notations on Mr. Hollister's 'Irony,' " *ibid.*, V, i (1965), 1-14; and C. Warren Hollister, "Reflections on the Unicorn's Head," *ibid.*, V, i (1965), 15-18.

BIBLIOGRAPHY

A good, fairly recent bibliography covering the Norman Conquest era of English history is Wilfrid Bonser, *An Anglo-Saxon and Celtic Bibliography (450–1087)* (2 vols., Berkeley and Los Angeles, 1957).